D0965452

# MAKE CHANGE

# MAKE CHANGE

How to Fight Injustice,
Dismantle Systemic Oppression,
and Own Our Future

## SHAUN KING

Houghton Mifflin Harcourt
Boston    New York
2020

For information about permission to reproduce selections from
this book, write to trade.permissions@hmhco.com or to Permissions,
Houghton Mifflin Harcourt Publishing Company, 3 Park Avenue,
19th Floor, New York, New York 10016.

hmhbooks.com

Library of Congress Cataloging-in-Publication Data is available.
ISBN 978-0-358-04800-8 (hardcover)
ISBN 978-0-358-04801-5 (ebook)

Book design by Emily Snyder

Printed in the United States of America
DOC 10 9 8 7 6 5 4 3 2 1

*To Zayah, Savannah, EZ, Kendi, Tae, and my dear Rai—*
*I love each of you so very much. Thanks for enduring all*
*it took for this book to be written with nothing but endless*
*love, patience, and encouragement.*

# Contents

# Foreword

Change never comes from the top down—it comes from the bottom on up. I first learned that lesson generations ago. I was just nineteen years old when I packed up to move out of Brooklyn to attend college at the University of Chicago. It was 1960, and the Civil Rights movement was growing all over the country. People were organizing in courageous ways against the despicable racism and bigotry that had become normalized in the United States.

At the University of Chicago, I became the chairman of the university chapter of CORE (Congress of Racial Equality), merged our group with SNCC (Student Nonviolent Coordinating Committee), and helped lead the very first sit-in on our campus against segregated student housing that was forcing my African American sisters and brothers to live in substandard conditions. Following our protests, the university formed a commission to address the problem and, in 1963, officially ended segregated student housing once and for all.

We didn't stop there. All over Chicago, while hundreds of classrooms at predominantly white public schools sat completely empty, young Black children were forced to go to class in overcrowded, dilapidated trailers. They were freezing cold during the winter and scorching hot in the sweltering Chicago summers. And so we organized. We chained ourselves to one another and put our bodies in front of the bulldozers standing by, ready to install more trailers for Black children. We were arrested and thrown in jail.

The problem of police brutality is not new. We organized against it when I was a student and blanketed the city with flyers demanding that it end. I remember the police coming right behind us and taking the flyers down as soon as we put them up. I was still a student when I became an organizer for the United Packinghouse Workers of America. They were early supporters of the courageous Montgomery Bus Boycott and had Dr. King as the keynote speaker at their annual convention in 1962. It was then, nearly sixty years ago, that I first truly understood that civil rights and workers' rights were one and the same.

During my life in public service, I have always believed that nothing is more powerful than the power of organizing. Our opponents have organized money, but organized money can be defeated by organized people—and this book is about how we can all throw our lives into organizing to make this world a better place together. Shaun understands that change does not just happen out of thin air. It's made.

It's crafted. It's organized. It's fought for. And when we fight together, we win.

It's not about me. It's not about Shaun. It's about us. If we are going to confront the reality that the United States incarcerates more people than any country in the history of the world, we must organize. If we are going to confront the reality that climate scientists are telling us that we have only a few years left to change the direction of our climate crisis, we must organize for a Green New Deal. The United States is the wealthiest country in the world, but on any given night, at least 553,000 men, women, and children are homeless and sleeping on our streets, 30 million people don't have health insurance, and 44 million Americans are drowning in student loan debt. Greed and corruption put us here, but we can organize so that every single American is housed, is insured, has their student loan debt forgiven, and is able to attend college for free. I truly believe we can do all of those things.

Brothers and sisters: We are in a time that can often feel frightening, but I am convinced that together we will not only endure it, but come through it better than we are today. Shaun and I still have hope in our future because we know that when ordinary people stand together and fight for justice, anything is possible.

Not only has Shaun helped organize on behalf of my campaigns, but together we have organized to elect brave new district attorneys. We have organized to support teachers' and workers' unions who went on strike for better wages and benefits. We have organized to hold corporations and billionaires accountable to pay their workers a living wage.

And through organizing, we have won great victories that we can and must build upon.

But now we need you. Join us. Or start your own cause or campaign, and we'll join you.

Of course, the naysayers, the corporate elite, and the billionaire class will try to deter and demoralize us, but we cannot let them. There is too much on the line for us to back down. We must commit ourselves to the hard work of organizing—and here's the good news: if we stand together, our nation's history tells us that there is nothing that we cannot accomplish.

*Bernie Sanders*

# Introduction

It was a beautiful, cloudless Friday morning in July of 2014. I could smell the ocean and hear the soothing sounds of its waves crashing as I took the first step out of my beat-up Hyundai and slammed the door shut. It was about 7 a.m., and Santa Monica was quiet. Rush-hour traffic in Los Angeles could be maddening, so I had left home super early that morning to beat the snarled highways and make my way to the offices of Global Green, an international environmental organization where I served as the director of communications. I was tempted, as I often was, to walk the extra block to the Pacific Coast Highway and stare out at the blue water that stretched as far as my eyes could see. Something about the ocean centers me. Seeing it never gets old. But I was behind on several tasks at work, and the mounting pressure of deadlines overruled my inclination to be contemplative that morning, so I made my way inside.

The job was a major change of pace for me after years of spearheading my own philanthropic projects. I had become known in charity circles for my use of social media and email listservs to build awareness and raise funds for causes, but doing it for an organization like Global Green was a new challenge, bringing me into a more corporate setting. As I climbed the steps to our cushy second-floor office, I had no expectation that this would be the day that would change the entire course of my life. Everything about it felt just like the day before, and the day before that, and the day before that. Routine. But as I reflect back on that day, and over my forty years on earth, I see my life as split in two, existing one particular way before that Friday and in an altogether different way after it.

For nearly a decade, Global Green had partnered with *Vanity Fair* to host its annual Oscars gala. The entire budget for the organization hinged on the success of the event. That morning, I organized our donor database, mundane but necessary work that consisted of cutting and pasting and entering data for hundreds of donors. As the hours crept along and my colleagues filed in, I received a push notification on my phone from a former classmate of mine from Morehouse, where I had attended college fifteen years earlier. It was a Facebook message.

"Shaun," my friend wrote. "Somebody posted something horrible on YouTube, man. The police are harassing this middle-aged brother on the street corner in New York and the dude is just begging them to leave him alone. He tells them over and over that he didn't do anything. The man wasn't armed. He wasn't violent. None of that. And all of a sudden, this plainclothes cop comes up behind him and starts choking the shit out of him, like UFC rear-naked-choke style. The cop chokes the man while the brother was still standing up — then wrestles him to the ground and continues choking him. And Shaun — you can hear the man yell out over and over and over again, 'I can't breathe — I can't breathe.' He says it a dozen times. And the guy dies right there on the sidewalk, man."

When I read those words, my stomach dropped. My first thought was that I couldn't click on that link in the Global Green office. Don't get me wrong: the people there were nice. But nobody ever talked about civil rights or police brutality or racial justice. I just didn't know if I was ready to explain to them what my friend told me I would be seeing. And I'm ashamed to admit this, but a small part of me thought that he must've left out a key detail somewhere along the way. What he described for me was cold-blooded murder in broad daylight, with witnesses, caught on film. I wondered whether my friend had left out an essential chunk of the story. He hadn't. Such videos have spread across the world in the years since, but before that day in July, a viral video of someone being killed by police simply did not exist, and so the reality of it was confounding.

I waited until my lunch break to watch the video, turning the volume down on my computer before clicking the link. What I saw was shocking. It was just as my friend had described, but worse ... much worse. The full video was roughly ten minutes long. I didn't yet know that the man's name was Eric Garner, or that this was in Staten Island, or that the cop who choked the man to death, Daniel Pantaleo, had been sued for his brutality three times before. I didn't know that police had been called there after a fight between some men in the neighborhood broke out, and that Eric Garner had actually served as a peacemaker during that situation. I didn't know that the police there had determined that, even though the fight was no longer going on, they needed to make an arrest of some kind anyway to fill their quotas. All I knew was that officers had surrounded this man, as if he was wanted for something truly dangerous. In the video, you hear as Eric Garner insists that he didn't do anything illegal, that he was minding his own business. But the police are undeterred. They claim they saw Garner selling a man a loosie, or a single cigarette, out of his pack. Since doing so was technically a criminal violation—albeit one that would produce nothing more than a ticket—they used that as their excuse to confront and arrest him.

When the video was shared on the news later, it was cut down to a fifteen-second clip, where you saw a man wrestled to the ground and heard him say "I can't breathe" over and over again. That was horrifying enough, but the thing that haunts me to this day is what they did not show: the moment Eric's body went limp. This vibrant, strong man who had done *nothing* to elicit such force went from saying "I am tired of being harassed" to gasping "I can't breathe" to total stillness and silence, in a matter of minutes. Shortly thereafter, the police, with no emotion or concern whatsoever, started poking at him like he was a dead animal. It was appalling. There was a profound disconnect between the physical reality of this Black man who had been choked to death, lying on the ground, and the casual manner of the officers afterward, as if it was business as usual.

I realized in that moment that, for the first time in my life, I had just witnessed a man die before my eyes. It felt unbelievable, like I was in a terrible dream. I was immediately reminded of the brutal choking death of a larger-than-life character named Radio Raheem in Spike Lee's classic film *Do the Right Thing*. But this wasn't the movies. This was real life, and an innocent man was dead because of baseless, unnecessary violence. Then an even more horrible realization overcame me: what I had just watched was the equivalent of a modern-day lynching. The brutality. The cruelty. The lack of justification for these actions. This was an unarmed, nonviolent man—a husband, a father, a son, a grandfather, someone whose life was taken away from him by an NYPD cop who served as judge, jury, and executioner that day. And the officers weren't the slightest bit pressed about it, even radioing one another on how Garner's death was no big deal to them. I had not yet heard the slogan "Black Lives Matter," but I remember feeling an internal rage at just how little the life of this beloved man meant to the police. Realizing this made my stomach turn, but it was not an altogether unfamiliar feeling.

Incidents of such gross brutality and violence had colored my consciousness for some time. From Emmett Till to Amadou Diallo to Sandra Bland to Trayvon Martin, there is a history in this country of unarmed, nonviolent Black men and women meeting brazen killers who refuse to value Black lives. But the difference here was that I had never seen any of those horrible murders with my own eyes. That afternoon, sitting in my cubicle, I watched a man literally breathe his last breath. Put simply, I was shook.

For the rest of the afternoon, I was completely unable to focus at work, my mind racing with ideas for how I could help get justice for this man and his family. My initial thought was simple and naive: if I found a way to share this video with my own network, a diverse group of individuals I'd known from years of fundraising, activism, and other social good activities, then it might eventually spread and catch the attention of the decision-makers and people in power, who would do something about it. Today that sounds really damn foolish, but sitting there at Global Green in July of 2014, it made sense to me. And so, straightaway, still in my cubicle, I began sharing clips of the video on my Facebook and Twitter pages, along with captions explaining that this man had essentially been lynched in broad daylight. The reaction was immediate, and it was deeply emotional. The mainstream media hadn't begun reporting this story yet, but the power of social media carried the news of Garner's death to thousands upon thousands of people. Soon enough, local news outlets in New York began covering it, with the *New York Daily News* putting it on their front page. A year later, I would be hired as their senior justice writer, in part because of the around-the-clock, hour-by-hour coverage I gave the case.

The case and the injustice of the murder of Eric Garner consumed me from that day forward. I took it personally, as if this had happened to a man I had called my friend. And so I went further down the rabbit hole, determined to excavate the truth. Instead of doing the work I was supposed to be doing for Global Green, I took that research and began channeling it into writing. Every single day, several times a day, I posted short pieces about the injustice of Eric Garner's murder on social media, breaking down the laws, demonstrating the facts of the situation via still photos and screenshots from the case, and explaining them in ways that everyday people could understand.

As the days passed and Eric Garner's killer still walked free, I began studying the legality of chokeholds by police and found that the NYPD had officially banned the move all the way back in 1993. That was twenty-one years prior to this incident, so in my mind it meant that the termination of Officer Daniel Pantaleo was imminent. This was captured on film, after all, and New York's own coroner's office had declared that Garner died by asphyxiation. But the more I dug into the NYPD's horrible history of choking Black people to death, the more I realized that the justice that I thought was around the corner wouldn't come without a fight. In spite of the practice being banned, more than two hundred complaints of chokeholds per year persisted inside the NYPD.

As Americans reeled from the public murder of Eric Garner, police violence continued all across the nation. Within three weeks of Eric Garner's murder, a young father named John Crawford III was shot and killed by police at a Walmart in Beavercreek, Ohio, near Dayton. Four days later, a teenage boy named Michael Brown was shot and killed in Ferguson, Missouri. And two days after that, a young man named Ezell Ford was shot and killed by police in Los Angeles. Police weren't killing people every few months, or even every few weeks, as I had thought, but every few *days*. We'd later find from the *Washington Post* database on police brutality that between 2015 and 2019, police have shot and killed an average of three people per day—nearly one thousand people per year—but at that moment there wasn't widespread awareness of the issue. These incidents would get trapped in the local news cycle, never getting national attention. I homed in on the injustice, determined to give these cases the voice they needed. I all but abandoned my responsibilities at Global Green, spending twelve-plus hours a day researching and writing pieces on police brutality. I finally left my job for good the next month, with no idea how I would provide for my family. It was so damn dumb of me, but I knew that we were in a moment that required all the energy I had to give. It was a movement without a name. We'd retrospectively call it the Black Lives Matter movement, but as it first grew from sparks in New York and Los Angeles and Ferguson, we were just scores of determined strangers prepared to fight back any way we knew how.

That was the turning point for me. I had fought against police brutality and white supremacy in the past; speaking and rallying and organizing were some of my most formative experiences as a young adult. But despite devoting so much of my early life to those things, after getting married and having five children, I had hung up the megaphone, for the most part. I never imagined that in the summer of 2014 my life and career would go back, in so many ways, to how I had started out as a young leader nearly twenty years earlier. All I knew was that watching Eric Garner served as a defibrillator to my conscience, propelling me to stop what I was doing and to fight against this profound injustice.

While I felt deep in my bones that our nation was experiencing a crisis, I didn't quite have the language or data to verbalize or quantify it. I'd soon come to understand that the police brutality we were witnessing was the worst it had been in the modern history of this country. But acts of violence were not just limited to incidents of police brutality. A public spike in all sorts of violent ideology and actions was spreading like a plague across our nation. Synagogues and mosques were being shot up. School shootings crescendoed to an all-time high. Hate crimes against the Black, Latinx, and LGBTQ communities skyrocketed. And a white nationalist would soon rise up and be elected president of the United States, setting forth a racist, xenophobic agenda under the guise of conservative values. I had no idea that any of that was coming when I began my earnest fight for justice, but it quickly became apparent to me that our nation's worst problems of the moment were deeply, deeply entrenched in the fabric of our society, with no end in sight.

I sometimes wonder whether my life would be where it is today had I not received that Facebook message from an old friend. I don't know if seeing it as a headline or reading about Eric Garner's murder as a trending topic later would've had the same effect as watching the horrors of that situation play out before my very eyes. All I know is that when it hit, instead of looking away, literally or figuratively, I decided to be a part of the solution, the fight, the struggle. I wrote this book not just to tell you all about my experiences in fighting for justice and freedom. I wrote this book because I want you to join me. The truth is that we just aren't effective alone. I need us to be in this struggle together.


Over the past few years, I've traveled to speak and organize in forty-five states. And in all of those places, the question I have received more than any other is some version of the following: "Shaun, what can I *actually* do about what's going on in the world to make an impact?"

I understand why so many people ask that question. Our worst problems seem increasingly permanent and irreversible, overwhelmingly so. Bigotry and racism and white supremacy are not some fading, fringe part of culture that will die once our elder generation passes away. These attitudes are everywhere. They are a youth movement. They are in the White House. They are deeply embedded in policies. The world is on fire, literally. Leading climate scientists have said that we have until 2030 to curb the rising temperature of the earth or the impact will be catastrophic. Mass shootings occur on what feels like a daily basis. Instead of being challenged or held to account, the world's worst dictators are being embraced by the American government. There is famine in Yemen and apartheid-like conditions in Palestine; up to two million Uighur Muslims have been detained in China. The news is a never-ending parade of catastrophe and despair.

Trying to capture the impact of this moment feels somewhat impossible, as every day brings its own unique horrors. Take, for instance, this forty-eight-hour snapshot of events that occurred in the middle of writing this book. In August of 2019, a white supremacist, whose manifesto echoed Donald Trump's tweets and all of the conservative propaganda about the "invasion" happening at the border between Mexico and the United States, opened fire at a Walmart in El Paso, Texas, killing twenty-two people and injuring twenty-six more. It was both gut-wrenching and terrifying, providing further evidence of our urgent need to credibly confront both white supremacy and gun reform in this nation. But before we could even really process what was happening, late that night, a gunman killed nine people and injured dozens more on the street in Dayton, Ohio.

With the nation in total despair, reeling in the wake of the successive mass shootings, three days later ICE raided several chicken-processing plants in rural Mississippi, arresting 680 Latinx workers. It was the largest mass arrest of immigrants in a single state in modern American history. The raids took place in small towns and at remote factories, mainly out of the view of journalists. Children were left alone at daycare and community centers, on the day before school was supposed to begin, with nobody to pick them up and take them home. Their guardians, their protectors, their caregivers—their most cherished loved ones—had been taken from them, leaving these little boys and girls alone and scared, with nowhere to go. A lone local journalist began photographing and filming the despondent children—heartbreaking images that showed these innocent children in various states of anguish and anxiety, often with their faces buried in their shirts or hands, overwhelmed by the cruelty they were facing.

In the middle of all this chaos, a journalist interviewed brave young Magdalena Gomez Gregorio, an eleven-year-old girl whose father was taken and detained in the raid. As she looked into the camera, choking out words between sobs, she told the reporter that her father was a good person, someone who had never been in trouble, and that now she had no idea how she'd eat or get the school supplies she was going to need the next day. The tears of these children had already broken me, but the courage of the young, grief-stricken Magdalena ripped me to shreds.

The next day, the following quote started circulating on social media:

> Terrible things are happening outside . . . poor helpless people are being dragged out of their homes . . . Families are torn apart; men, women and children are separated. Children come home to find that their parents have disappeared.

These words were written by Anne Frank on January 13, 1943, but the brutal truth is that Magdalena Gomez Gregorio could've written them herself. While it feels almost impossible to believe that a sentiment expressed during one of the most inhumane moments in history could be relevant in this era, it damn sure is. The actions of ICE may have been legal, but what we retrospectively come to call crimes against humanity almost always are. And it's the increased frequency of these inhumane attacks that makes our current environment so overwhelming. But it is essential that we fight back. As we grieve and try to keep ourselves from falling off the cliff into a place of total despair, we must also find a way to move from desperation to organization. And while that's no easy pivot, our very survival depends on our doing this together.

That's why I wrote this book. I don't say this lightly, but I think we have a national case of PTSD. We have experienced so much trauma and loss as a country, and so little justice and healing, that it is understandable that we're in a fog, struggling to find our way forward. I'm not telling you to "shake it off" — it's never that easy — but I *am* telling you that, while we are frozen and in a daze, the people and systems and corporations that mean us harm are not. They are marching forward. Every problem that ails us continues because of their relentless commitment to the status quo. I want to help you, to help *us*, understand that we are facing threats and enemies and obstacles that will not disappear just because we really, really want them to. We must chart a path and march forward as if our very lives depend on it — because in this era, they do.

For years, I thought I knew what making change looked and felt like. I was wrong. And I don't mean that I was wrong once or twice; I was wrong several times before I finally accepted that my working philosophy of changemaking was fatally flawed. It wasn't my heart that led me in the wrong direction — that was always in the right place, and I'm sure yours is, too. But we can all have the best of intentions, and still fail in our pursuit of justice and progress if we don't truly understand how meaningful, system-disrupting change is made.

That's what this book is about. It's the story of how I fought so hard for change and failed miserably for years on end. It's the story of how I finally came to accept that it wasn't just the might of our enemies but the design of our strategies that keeps us losing. It's the story of how we finally started winning in our fight for real, substantive, systemic change when we shifted our methods and targets. It's a book about how my hope in our future was restored, even in the midst of unthinkable bigotry and violence, because I finally saw a real path to victory for us. And most of all, it's a book about how *you* can make change, because if I know one thing, it's that it's going to take every single one of us moving in the same direction, at the same time, and in a deeply organized way, if we are going to shape this world into a beautiful vision that is so much better than what we're seeing and living through right now.

*Part One*

# Our Roots, My Roots

W HEN YOU PICKED UP this book, you picked up
a pass to a better future for yourself and for
this world. At my heart, I am an imaginative futurist,
and I absolutely believe we have the power to build and
own what our future becomes. To do that, though, we
need to reflect on some key lessons from the past that
will shine a bright light on the steps ahead.

In order to be an effective change agent, you need
to understand two things: where we are in history and
how you, personally, can have an impact. In chapter 1,
we are going to go macro and examine how we think
about time and social progress as compared to the reality of how human history actually unfolds. This chapter is the key, the legend, the guide that is going to inform the rest of the decisions and action steps I am
going to encourage you to take throughout the rest of

this book. In chapter 2, I am going to tell you my personal origin story. I'm going to be vulnerable and put all of my business out there, showing you my scars and wounds, so that you can understand how these experiences shaped my activism. In the pages ahead, I am going to ask you to dig deep into your past, too, in order for you to make key decisions about how you will fight for change. It's going to be a difficult, soul-searching experience, but I promise you, it'll be worth it. Are you ready? Let's jump in.

# 1

# The Dip

IT'S HARD TO FULLY understand a moment in history when you are in it.

Let me rephrase that: it's damn near *impossible* to understand and appreciate a historical moment or era when you are living in it. It's just not something you notice or think about as you go about your day. Our everyday lives, even amid the chaos of the world, are exceedingly mundane. We eat, sleep, shower, shit, work, laugh a little, make some love, and do so every single day with full knowledge that parts of the world are crumbling all around us.

Now, when the history books are written, the eating, sleeping, showering, shitting, working, laughing, and making love are completely removed. As far as they are concerned, nobody has ever had to piss in all of human history; no woman has ever been on her period; nobody has had to pay a bill or wait in line at the DMV or get their hair cut.

History books have a way of erasing everything that makes us fully human. They skip from highlight to highlight and crisis to crisis, but that's not actually how time unfolds.

Time is full of heartache and heartburn. It's full of laundry and meal planning. It's full of traffic and charging your phone and rushing to work and being glad to get home in the evening after a long day. And in the middle of it all, when groundbreaking, earth-shattering historical events take place, it's hard to know what they truly mean in the context of history, because, well, you also need to take the garbage out and do the dishes, and your health insurance is expensive as hell, and you have no idea how you're going to pay off your student loans. Our real lives look and feel nothing like the history books, and so, over and over again, from the beginning of time until now, humans have found themselves caught in the middle of catastrophic genocide and war, dictatorial fascism and bigotry, without an intuitive understanding of how we got there.

As a high school student, when I studied World War II and learned about the sheer devastation of the Holocaust, I was utterly confused as to how the entire world allowed millions of people to be rounded up, snatched from their homes and jobs and communities, separated from their loved ones, forced to work, and then murdered en masse. In the history books I read, the Holocaust lacked a comprehensive preface: Hitler simply came to power in the chapter following the Great Depression and *boom*, there we were, in midst of evil. But that's not how it really happened. None of history's worst moments happen all of a sudden. There are always warning signs. You don't wake up one day to find yourself suddenly exposed to genocide or war or famine or fascism; it creeps up on you, moment by moment, day by day, until you are fully immersed in it, surrounded on all sides.

As a kid, when I thought ahead to the future, my dreams were nothing but hopeful. I never could've imagined how many horrible turns our world would take. How is it that we live in the deadliest era for gun violence in American history? How could the United States now be listed as one of the ten most dangerous countries in the world for women and the fifth most dangerous country in the world for journalists? How could Donald Trump win the presidency one month after a tape recording was released of him proudly bragging about walking up to women, forcefully kissing them, and grabbing them by their genitals? How is it possible, in this day and age, that children who arrive at our border as refugees are being ripped from their mothers' arms and separated, sometimes by thousands of miles, not for safety but for cruelty and nothing more?

I don't think you'd dispute that we are in a deeply problematic place right now. It's awful. And when so many depraved things happen in such rapid succession, it's easy to get lost in and overwhelmed by the hopelessness of it all. When we get stuck in the malaise of these moments, without examining their root causes, it starts to feel like quicksand. We must look forward, yes, but neglecting the truths of the past will doom us to repeat them. Because if we don't *really* understand how we got here, then how do we escape it?

———

I don't get down often, but in January of 2015, I found myself in an unfamiliar place of gloom and dread. A cloud was over me and I just couldn't shake it. I had left a reliable job to throw my entire life into seeking justice for families who had lost a loved one to police brutality—and we were getting nothing close to that outcome.

It was brutal, grueling, emotionally draining work. From the beginning of the Black Lives Matter movement, the pace had been that of a full sprint, with little time for recovery or reflection between incidents. Daily, I would be asked to support and advocate for someone else who had experienced a new atrocity at the hands of the police. I'm thinking of men and women like Dontre Hamilton, Akai Gurley, Yvette Smith, Ernest Satterwhite, Tanisha Anderson—all of whom were unarmed when they were killed by the police. I would try my best to swiftly assess the facts of each case, while also responding quickly enough to break into the news cycle. By this time, I was writing several pieces a day for the *Daily Kos*, which gave me a national platform, and that platform meant that more and more heartbroken pleas for help were flooding my inbox. Today we have dozens of local and national reporters whose beat is social justice or even police brutality specifically, but in 2014, few such positions existed. I saw my primary responsibility as providing color, shape, and nuance to the very real pain being experienced by victims of police violence. These families were being pulled in a thousand different directions by dueling relatives, politicians, attorneys, journalists, and public safety officials. For each of them, it must have been like the fog of war. I found myself in the position of not only telling their stories but providing them with the guidance and support they needed. I'd recommend and introduce them to civil attorneys; I'd raise funds for funerals and family support; I'd connect them with local and national organizers who I thought could help. Straightaway, I blurred the lines between journalist and activist, with one foot in each world.

The more I came to know and love so many of these families, the harder I fought for them to get justice. As a former pastor, I had visited and comforted countless families through moments of despair, but this was different. Having a family member shot and killed by police proved to be a unique kind of pain to experience and endure. Imagine that the government that you pay to protect you has murdered someone you cherish, and then imagine that as a result of that brutal injustice, people now expect you to get on a microphone, or in front of cameras, and say something of substance. It's a strange kind of loss and an abnormal pressure for any suffering person to experience. Instead of simply being able to grieve, these families impacted by police violence were expected to march, make smart legal decisions, filter through scores of people offering help, and somehow muster up enough strength to demand justice.

Inspired by these families' bravery, and armed with more and more information about the prevalence of police violence, people all over the country began to organize. #BlackLivesMatter quickly moved from a hashtag and trending topic to a full-fledged mantra and movement, with people demanding justice through protests, marches, and demonstrations. The movement was not one organization but hundreds, created in all fifty states and on college campuses all over the country. Social media obliterated the traditional parameters for civil rights organizing, providing a platform where one did not need permission or privilege to speak or organize. Women and queer folks had always been indispensable in previous movements, but they had frequently been wedged into private organizing roles; now they were at the forefront, both online and off, leading people in fresh new ways. These actions took over entire cities and college campuses across the United States and abroad; they shut down highways and blocked offices and interrupted day-to-day routines to bring attention to the cause. People were putting their bodies and their freedom on the line. And even though the protests in Ferguson and beyond were fierce and contentious, the prevailing sentiment on the ground was still one of hope. For the first time in my entire life, the widespread brutality of police officers was being examined and scrutinized the way it deserved. The oppressed were being heard. They were being seen. And to people whose pain is so often treated like it's invisible, being heard and seen felt like progress.

Then, on the afternoon of Saturday, November 22, 2014, the bottom fell out. I don't know if I'd call it "the day I lost all hope," but it was damn sure the day I started losing it. After four straight months of protests and around-the-clock media coverage of the crisis of police brutality, something truly shocking occurred. Just a few blocks from his mother's house on the west side of Cleveland, Ohio, a twelve-year-old boy named Tamir Rice was playing outside of his neighborhood rec center with his big sister when a squad car from the Cleveland Police Department came barreling off the street and onto the grass of the park. Before the car even came to a complete stop, Officer Timothy Loehmann yelled through the closed window for the boy to put his hands up. Unbeknownst to Tamir, a white man had called 911 to report that he was playing with what appeared to be a toy gun; when the information was dispatched to the police, they reported the call as a man with an actual gun. As Tamir got up off a park bench to see what the problem was, the officer shot him center mass. This all happened within seconds of the car pulling up. When Tamir's sister, just fourteen years old herself, came running to check on her little brother, understandably distraught, police responded by tackling her to the ground, handcuffing her, and putting her in the police car parked just feet away from her dying brother. As Tamir moaned in pain, the officers ignored him, offering him no comfort, kind words, or medical assistance. Nothing. He was just a baby. A prankster who still watched cartoons and imagined he'd be a basketball star one day. Imagine yourself at that age.

That was devastating enough, but over the next month matters got worse and worse. Two days after Tamir was murdered, a public announcement was made that no charges were going to be filed against Ferguson police officer Darren Wilson in the shooting death of Michael Brown. The case was being closed, no wrongdoing found. A week later, conservative Staten Island district attorney Daniel Donovan made the exact same announcement about NYPD officer Daniel Pantaleo. Even though Eric Garner's murder had been filmed and the city's medical examiner had ruled that his death was caused by "a lethal cascade of events" resulting from the banned chokehold, no charges were going to be filed. The same was determined in the shooting death of John Crawford III. Each announcement only compounded the utter devastation felt by the families and communities that had hoped against hope that they would be the exception to the rule. Around that time, we learned that Loehmann's bosses at his previous job had questioned his competence and had actually recommended that he be let go after he exhibited a pattern of emotional instability. For the first time in my life, I fully understood rioting. I understood burning shit down. I felt that very energy boiling over in my own heart. Justice would have been the release that the nation needed, but it was being denied again and again.

I don't know why I had fooled myself into thinking that we were going to get justice for any of those families, considering the United States' historical treatment of African Americans, but I swear to you, I thought it was a real possibility. Shortly after Tamir was murdered, amid these announcements, I got a call from my friend Tory Russell. He had been a relentless frontline protester and organizer in Ferguson, and had traveled up to Cleveland to meet with Tamir's family to offer them his support and guidance. They were dejected, overwhelmed, and bewildered. Tory put Tamir's uncle on the phone, and I said to him what I would say to countless families over the next two years. As confident as I was that $2 + 2 = 4$, I told him, "Don't worry. Hang in there. We're going to get justice for your family." Not a single fiber in my being thought an incompetent police officer who never should've been hired in the first place could get away with shooting and killing a sweet twelve-year-old boy. When police released the surveillance video of Tamir being shot and killed, it was basically like watching a drive-by shooting, a cruelty only compounded by the footage that showed the officers idly letting him suffer on the cold concrete in his final moments. In viewing that horrible footage, I saw what I thought was an open-and-shut case. And in a twisted way, it was: not a single charge was filed against the officers. Nothing. Not a criminal negligence or reckless homicide charge, not even a misdemeanor. Hell, they didn't even receive a ticket for the whole damn thing. Not only was the family expected to pay for Tamir's funeral and burial, but the City of Cleveland had the audacity to send the family a bill for the emergency services rendered.

With each case that was closed, it wasn't just a headline or trending topic for those of us involved in the Black Lives Matter movement—it was a deep, painful, personal rejection. As police unions all over the country rallied behind the officers who murdered these boys and men, wearing T-shirts mocking the victims and holding online fundraisers for the officers, I felt like I was witnessing the massive white crowds who once gathered, smiled, and posed for pictures in front of charred, dangling lynched bodies of Black men, women, and children. These people were proud; they were reveling in their victory. White power was still fully intact. And so the families who were ruined by this wave of police violence were left to pick up all the pieces of their lives, with no hope whatsoever to try and balance the scales for what happened to their loved ones. In the Old Testament, if you took an eye, you lost an eye. If you took an arm, you lost an arm. If you took a son, you lost a son. Here, though, the families weren't asking for eyes or arms or sons — they just wanted the state to acknowledge and recognize their wrong and dole out some semblance of punishment for it. Yet over and over again, the system denied them anything of the sort.

The overwhelming lack of justice flattened me. From a young age, I had been taught that whatever I fought for and worked for and set my mind upon, if I gave it my all, I'd accomplish it. It sounds so damn simple now as I share that with you, but for most of my life, that had been true. As a student leader, I never lost an election. As a fundraiser, I always hit my goal. Damn near every job I ever applied for, I got. And I sincerely believed that throwing my absolute all into fighting for justice for these families, working alongside countless other women and men who were doing the exact same thing, meant that we'd get some version of justice. We didn't.

I began to question everything I believed about my role and the actual value of my contributions. I knew that the decks were unfairly stacked against us as we pursued justice for these families, but with each officer who was protected, the reality grew starker. I realized that I had overpromised and underdelivered in a major way to so many families. And the fact that I was becoming more and more known around the world as an activist and journalist only served to compound my guilt. I loathed the fame. Everywhere I went, whether to get gas, to run errands, to eat a meal, people would recognize me. They were nothing but kind and complimentary, but I didn't do the work to get famous — I did it to get justice. I avoided public interviews, awards, media appearances, and celebrity hobnobbing like the plague. The newfound public recognition had stressed my family out in the worst possible way. The sole justification I gave my wife and our kids, my mother and brother, for the costs they were now paying for me being someone in the public eye was the fact that I was going to be able to leverage this somehow to get justice for these families who so badly deserved it. When that didn't happen, and we began getting death threats daily, it became clear that I had put my entire family through hell for goals that we just weren't going to achieve. In some ways, I felt like a famous failure, and became increasingly withdrawn around my family and friends.

By then, I was writing about injustice daily for the *Daily Kos,* but I wondered if I was even on the right path. In just a few months, I wrote hundreds of articles and reports for them. But I didn't just want to *document* injustice, although doing so is critically important—I wanted to *stop* it. I had already enrolled in a master's in history program at Arizona State University in hopes of sharpening my mind and preparing to eventually earn a PhD, but I barely made it through my first semester. I was struggling mightily under the weight of trying to organize against injustice alongside my job as a journalist and the responsibilities inherent in raising a family with five young kids. All over my world, I was dropping balls and pissing off supervisors, allies, and friends as I stumbled through everything. Taking a leave of absence from school seemed like the smartest thing to do, but my wife, who was in grad school herself, wasn't having it. She had seen me start and stop grad school before and wasn't going to allow me to do it again.

When I started the next semester, in January 2015, with an Introduction to Historiography course, it took me about thirty seconds to realize that I had made a huge mistake. The professor began the class by showing a large black-and-white drawing of a long-haired, bearded white man—think Gandalf of *The Lord of the Rings* or Dumbledore from *Harry Potter*, but even older and without the magic. It was the famous nineteenth-century German historian Leopold von Ranke, known as "the father of modern history." I felt myself getting angry as I stared at his portrait. I could not imagine that von Ranke had anything to say that would be even remotely useful or relevant to the current movement for civil and human rights. It wasn't because he was old or white or German that I assumed it was highly unlikely that von Ranke's perspective was going to be of service to me or the thousands of us who were starting to form real bonds in the fight for justice. It was just that my life was so centered in the living, breathing reality of that moment that I could not imagine that von Ranke's experiences centuries prior could help me wade through the modern waters of police brutality and mass incarceration. What did he know about our modern systems of racism or bigotry? What did he know about confronting capitalism, patriarchy, or systemic oppression?

I literally don't remember anything else from the class that day. I was done, had checked out. The next day, I started researching what I had to do to drop the course and replace it with a different one. I didn't realize it at the time, but college students all over the country would later tell me that during this same period, they, too, had struggled to focus and feel like their coursework was even remotely relevant. It's hard to concentrate when you feel like the whole world is crashing down around you.

Now, I don't know how it was for you in school, but my grad school program only had two or three woke professors — and those classes always filled up right away. So when I started clicking around on the college registrar's website to see what else was available, the only possible replacements were classes like Advanced Badminton. Unfortunately, you needed to have taken Intro to Badminton to register for that one, so I had no choice but to stay in Intro to Historiography. Had one of a dozen different courses been open to me, I would've dropped that class like a bad habit. But, as fate would have it, I was destined to be in it and couldn't shake it if I wanted to.

And you know what? I am so thankful for that, because what I learned in that class and specifically from Leopold von Ranke ended up being the single most important lesson of my entire academic career. It changed my life. It informed how I would come to understand the brutal murders of Freddie Gray and Sandra Bland later that year. It informed how I saw and understood the senseless killings of Philando Castile, Terence Crutcher, and Alton Sterling in 2016, and of the brilliant student athlete Jordan Edwards in 2017, among countless others. It shaped how I saw the egregious spike in hate crimes all over the United States in the wake of the 2016 election of Donald Trump. It colored how I saw the public demonstration of bigotry in the 2017 Unite the Right march on Charlottesville, Virginia, which left one brave woman dead and dozens more brutally injured. It informed how I saw the incident in which two courageous men gave their lives to protect a Muslim woman from a bigot on a train in Portland, Oregon. It changed how I understood the tragic death of Nia Wilson in Oakland, California. It changed how I saw the Muslim ban, the brutal assassination of *Washington Post* journalist Jamal Khashoggi, the MAGA bomber, and the mass shootings in places like Orlando and Las Vegas. This book simply wouldn't exist without that class.

What I soon learned was that Leopold von Ranke's work was not only timeless—it was actually about time itself. Let me explain. Most modern historians are topical experts. Some historians may focus their entire careers on the life and work of one individual leader, while others may focus on certain technological advancements or particular wars or social movements. But Leopold von Ranke set out to compile the first exhaustive, detailed, annotated timeline of world history. In doing so, he became widely known as the father of source-based history. Von Ranke's pioneering work on this timeline, alongside his establishment of essential college training programs for historians, cemented his place as a forever leader in the field.

Today, news about the world can be gathered with the click of a button, but von Ranke had none of those resources at his nineteenth-century disposal. Imagine a world with no internet. No television. No iPhones or Androids. No cable news. No telephones. In fact, homes did not yet even have electricity. The entire planet was unplugged and analog, which meant that the distribution of information and knowledge was hyperlocal.

Von Ranke had embarked on a mammoth task. His mission was to chart human history, from ancient civilizations all the way up to his modern time, noting every hero, villain, warlord, politician, artist, author, inventor, military leader, royal family member, revolutionary, icon, trendsetter, and celebrity, as well as all of the movements, periods, eras, changes, and shifts that they each birthed and lived through. It was a tedious and massive undertaking that required him to travel to churches, courthouses, and libraries throughout Europe, gathering documents and taking meticulous notes from firsthand sources and historical records. He then placed everything in chronological order, mapping it out, to see if there were any consistent trends in human behavior over time.

What he found shocked him. Von Ranke, like many leading thinkers of the day, fully believed in the idea of evolutionary history and humanity, which is the notion that from the beginning of time as we know it until now, human beings have consistently evolved and improved. Von Ranke's contemporary, Charles Darwin, published his groundbreaking work *On the Origin of Species* in 1859, at the same time von Ranke was doing his best work. The core idea of Darwin's theory was that over time, through competition and natural selection, human beings improve; the species positively evolves. Von Ranke believed this as well—until he began to see that history itself did not bear that out.

When von Ranke began building out this timeline in the 1880s, he noticed something very peculiar. Looking over thousands of years of human history, from the end of the prehistoric age up until the 1450s, instead of the quality of humanity being in a steady upward, progressive trajectory, von Ranke found that human beings perpetually alternated back and forth between improvement and regression, peace and war, provision and famine, unity and dissension, freedom and captivity, good and evil. If you were to put the patterns of humanity that von Ranke found on a graph, the timeline would look like the Himalayas, with jagged, harsh peaks where humanity improved, followed by plummets into the deepest, darkest valleys imaginable. Then press repeat. Over and over again. Progress. Failure. Progress. Failure. Progress. Failure. Without actually uttering the old adage "History repeats itself," von Ranke proved that very thing.

It's understandable why the notion that human beings are steadily getting better over time has prevailed—it's because, for the longest time, we have confused our deep desire for the steady improvement of humanity with the *actual* steady improvement of technology over time. In my lifetime alone, the technology behind phones has gone from something stuck to the wall to a small computer that you carry in your pocket. It's that way for so many other things as well, from the way we listen to music to how we get our news to how we travel from place to place. It's easy to look at those steady improvements in technology and confuse them with the steady improvement of society, but these concepts aren't one and the same. What we have failed to fully grasp is that our gadgets, our things, our creations, can get faster, more complex, and more affordable over time without that having even the slightest impact on the *quality of our humanity*. Faster internet speed does not mean we are quicker to be kind. Clearer, larger television screens do not help us understand the depths of our problems any better. While the inevitable forward march of technology is on one path, humanity is marching to the beat of an altogether different drummer.

Most U.S. history textbooks teach students a form of progressive evolutionary history, thereby instilling in all of us the belief that we, as citizens of the United States, are steadily improving and growing and becoming better people. But when American history is told in a way that goes from beautiful highlight to beautiful highlight, we are left with a narrative that falls somewhere between propaganda and a lie. It's the Instagramification of American history —where bad news and setbacks are rarely mentioned and we all just post our most beautiful selfies and pictures and videos of kittens, sunsets, and tasty food. Those things are a part of your real life, sure, but they aren't a sincere representation of life itself.

Von Ranke helped me understand that if we only acknowledge, record, and celebrate historical highlights, then we are simply not seeing an accurate, full picture of human history. It's a gross distortion. But it's absolutely the norm. The general consensus has long since been that the United States is on a strong progressive, positive incline, in that the 2000s were better than the nineties, which were better than the seventies, which were better than the fifties, and so on. And when we have this type of evolutionary view of history, we end up feeling duped when terrible things happen.

Sometime in the summer of 2015, I began to notice an interesting phenomenon in conversations and on the internet. I first picked up on it that June, after a white supremacist named Dylann Roof walked into a small-group Bible study and prayer meeting being held at the historic Emanuel African Methodist Episcopal Church in Charleston, South Carolina. He was out of place—a quiet, withdrawn white man, a stranger, in an intimate Bible study of nothing but close Black friends. Skeptical or not, it was the tradition of the church—and of almost all Black churches—to accept the presence of an outsider. Within minutes Roof shot and killed the pastor, Clementa Pinckney, and eight other faithful men and women who had gathered together in that room. Long before the news of the shooting hit network news, it began spreading on social media. And all over Twitter—which, in the absence of any Black news network, had to fill in the gaps of what had happened in Charleston—I saw tweets that said things like "It feels like we're going back in time," "I swear this feels like some old school KKK shit," and "What is this, the 1960s?"

The same thing happened when white supremacists descended upon Charlottesville on August 11, 2017. Men marched through the city with torches, chanting "Jews will not replace us," and when one of these bigots got behind the wheel, he killed a young woman and seriously injured dozens of others. I lost count of the number of times I saw people ask some version of "How could this be happening in 2017?" The expectation was that we had progressed to a place and a time where such things would no longer happen, a miscalculation that did not properly account for the wild and painful pendulum swings that history frequently takes.

If we take the von Ranke approach to time and history and

honestly lay out every moment—good, bad, and ugly—on a timeline of American history, a very different story than one of steady, predictable growth and progress emerges. Instead we see that with American history, like all human history, humanity consistently experiences peaks and valleys, soaring highs and unbelievable lows. And when humankind does improve in beautiful ways, it does not mean that it will remain that way, or get better. The only sure bet is that human beings will swing back and forth between their best and worst instincts.

Those low periods are what I refer to as *the dip*. Dips in human history are where we see deep systemic widespread suffering and oppression, where we find genocide and famine, slavery and war. It's where codified bigotry and inequality become woven into society, where oppression is not just legalized but *normalized*. The dip is where bigotry, hatred, and violence are so routine that they become background noise in our society. And let me tell you this: these dips do not appear at random. Not at all. When a historic moment, be it a war or a movement that produces a sweeping new set of policies, interrupts the status quo—and particularly if it displaces or is perceived to threaten the people who hold the power—a drastic dip almost always follows. It's like clockwork. Let me explain.

Until 1863, property owners in the United States of America were in the business of buying, selling, and trading human beings, then forcing them to work as slaves from birth until death. It's one of the most despicable periods in all of human history. The U.S. economy was built on the backs of this free, forced labor. At least ten of the first fifteen American presidents owned human beings. The first president, George Washington, had a mouthful of teeth taken from some of the hundreds of slaves he owned. Enslaved Africans literally helped build and expand Washington, D.C. Any nation that has an economy driven by free labor has a high likelihood of explosive growth, and so the American economy boomed, at the expense of its integrity and humanity.

The American Civil War disrupted all of this. The Emancipation Proclamation and the Thirteenth, Fourteenth, and Fifteenth Amendments effectively ended slavery and granted equal rights to all Americans. Of course, we now know that the Thirteenth Amendment has a clause that allows slavery to continue for those who are incarcerated, but the truth remains that the Civil War brought the single biggest shift in American history seen up until that point. And to say that ending slavery disturbed the people in power is an understatement of epic proportions. Within just a few years, formerly enslaved African Americans rose to political power, winning more than two thousand elections across the country in the years between 1866 and 1877, also known as Reconstruction. It was a period of momentous, groundbreaking change. Sixteen African Americans were elected to Congress. In 1870, Hiram Revels, of Mississippi, became the first Black person elected to the U.S. Senate. Blanche Bruce followed him with a full term that began in 1875. Six hundred African Americans rose to power and were elected to state legislatures across the country, including in states like South Carolina, Mississippi, and Louisiana.

But these gains were short-lived. A dip soon followed, one that was grotesque and massive in its scope.

Come 1877, the era of Reconstruction was replaced by occurrences of brutal lynching and discrimination that unto themselves constituted a unique new kind of horror. To study this era is to see the gross contradictions of the American justice system. In reality, more laws not only existed but were enforced to protect enslaved Africans before 1863 than there were to protect these same individuals after emancipation. Can you guess why? It's because, while enslaved Africans were not valued as human beings, they were valued as a financial investment. When that lone financial value was stripped away and African Americans rose to power, the collective ire of white America came down on this newly freed population in the worst ways. Not hundreds but thousands upon thousands of Black men, women, and children—sometimes entire families—were murdered and maimed, hung and burned, all over the country. The political power shifted, too: after Blanche Bruce finished his single term in the Senate, the nation would not elect another African American senator for eighty-five years. In spite of what appeared to be newfound constitutional voting protections, those rights were routinely infringed upon throughout the nation. Racist codes and policies were developed requiring Black voters to do impossibly foolish tasks like guessing the number of bubbles in a bar of soap or reciting obscure laws in full to have the right to cast a ballot. And suddenly, everyday behavior in the Black community became criminalized, ranging from standing in one location for too long or talking too loud to walking after dark. Farmland that Black folk had cultivated for generations was routinely stolen without compensation. African

Americans, who were briefly on pace to recover and gain power after slavery, were forced into a new type of terror and subjugation called Jim Crow.

From 1878 until the late 1960s, segregation and normalized legal inequality became the status quo in the United States. WHITES ONLY signs were the norm not just for water fountains but in thousands of restrooms, restaurants, buses, trains, and businesses. From 1881 to 1967, not a single Black senator was elected in the country. Voting rights were effectively stolen as hundreds of thousands of eligible Black voters were routinely stripped from the rolls by any means necessary—including the literal discarding of voter registrations. And even if your name was not stripped, poll taxes, tests, and threats of violence reduced Black voting to effectively zero in many counties in the South. In reaction to this, an innovative social awakening aimed at shaking up that horrible new status quo began picking up real momentum: the Civil Rights movement. Its leaders started using brave new methods to directly confront segregation, bigotry, and inequality, from sitting in at lunch counters to registering people to vote. Before this era, with few exceptions, the costs of fighting back for civil and human rights were so severe that mass marches, protests, boycotts, demonstrations, and confrontations in the South were virtually nonexistent. But when civil rights leaders took the risk, bringing entire communities with them, they exerted strength in numbers, and the philosophy of direct nonviolent resistance began achieving goals and victories all across the nation. And out of that movement came groundbreaking Supreme Court decisions and laws, from *Brown v. Board of*

*Education* (1954) to the Civil Rights Act of 1964 and the Voting Rights Act of 1965.

We could debate just how much all of those laws and decisions produced, but this much is clear: the advancements of the Civil Rights movement disturbed the primary people in power, and, as a result, violence toward African Americans and their allies skyrocketed. President John F. Kennedy and his brother Robert, the former attorney general, were assassinated, as were leading organizers and leaders of the movement, from Medgar Evers to Dr. Martin Luther King Jr. Four little girls were murdered by a bomb in their Birmingham church. Three young men—James Chaney, Andrew Goodman, and Michael Schwerner—who were part of Freedom Summer, a coordinated campaign to combat Black disenfranchisement, were killed for their work helping to register Black voters. And those are just a few of the more well-known stories. There are countless others who made sacrifices. Consider just a few of these unsung heroes: Reverend George Lee was murdered in 1955 in Mississippi for registering people to vote. Three months later, a Black man named Lamar Smith was shot dead on the courthouse lawn by a white man for registering people to vote in Brookhaven, Mississippi. In 1961, Herbert Lee, known for registering Black voters, was shot and killed; three years later, the only witness to that murder, Louis Allen, was also shot and killed. In 1966, Vernon Dahmer offered to pay the poll taxes that were prohibiting people from voting in Mississippi. His home was firebombed and he was burned to death. Wharlest Jackson, an NAACP leader in Natchez, Mississippi, died when a bomb was set off in his car in February of 1967. Those are just a few martyrs to the cause who don't get the recognition they deserve, and whose stories demonstrate just how dangerous it was to fight for change.

Put simply, the United States did not welcome the shifts of the fifties and sixties with open arms. The gains of the movement had to be forced upon this nation through the difficult, brutal, and dangerous work described above. But because these brave men and women persevered, a dip, a backlash, was guaranteed to follow. The primary people in power are never disturbed and threatened without a response, and so we moved into a new era of scrutiny.

With African Americans now fully guaranteed voter protections for the first time in American history, the next dip in the quality of humanity was introduced by none other than President Richard Nixon. It was eventually called the war on drugs, but his domestic policy chief, John Ehrlichman, made it clear that it was always meant to be a war on people. Few people knew Nixon as intimately as Ehrlichman. Not only did he work side by side with the president during his administration, but Ehrlichman was part of Nixon's unsuccessful 1960 presidential campaign and his failed attempt to run for governor in California two years later. He was well aware of Nixon's policies and his attitudes, in other words.

Here's what Ehrlichman said about that contrived war:

You want to know what this was really all about? The Nixon campaign in 1968, and the Nixon White House after that, had two enemies: the antiwar left and black people. You understand what I'm saying? We knew we couldn't make it illegal to be either against the war or black, but by getting the public to associate the hippies with marijuana and blacks with heroin, and then criminalizing both heavily, we could disrupt those communities. We could arrest their leaders, raid their homes, break up their meetings, and vilify them night after night on the evening news. Did we know we were lying about the drugs? Of course we did.

And there we have it—the single, most definitive admission that the war on drugs was never about drugs, but about criminalizing and vilifying very specific groups of people. And while white hippies had the luxury of simply cutting their hair or changing their clothes to avoid being targeted, African Americans would always be Black, and would soon become the primary victims of an explosion of mass incarceration. That shift did not occur as a response to drugs or to violence; it was initiated by the government to stunt the growing political and economic power of a people benefiting from the gains of the Civil Rights movement.

I often hear people say that America's criminal justice system is "broken," and I understand that thought. Something clearly is wrong, and "broken" seems to be as good a word as any. But to say that the justice system in the United States is broken is to suggest that the explosion of mass incarceration from the Nixon administration onward was some type of grand accident—that the system was well designed but, for some strange reason, has deviated from its original intent. And that's just not the case. This system was built deliberately with nefarious goals in mind. It was intended not only to protect white power and privilege, but to disrupt and punish Black communities in the worst ways imaginable. That system isn't broken, no. It's firing on all cylinders.

The statistics back this up. For most of American history, the total number of incarcerated men and women was consistently below 200,000. But in the middle of the twentieth century, that all changed. The Nixon administration decided to declare a war on drugs to destabilize and criminalize Blackness itself. Read that quote again. John Ehrlichman openly admitted that they knew they could not make it illegal to be Black, so they found a creative workaround. The war on drugs abused existing laws, selectively enforcing them, with ferocity, almost exclusively in Black communities. Consequently, from 1968 until today, the number of people in American jails and prisons has exploded to more than twelve times what it was throughout most of the first half of the twentieth century. On top of all of this, scores of new laws, particularly for probation and parole, were created with the intent of selectively enforcing them in communities of color. Consider this: For each person in jail or prison, there are currently two others on probation or parole. Black Americans are 3.5 times as likely as whites to be one of those on supervisory probation. And annually, more than 350,000 people are sent back to prison—many of whom simply fail to meet the stringent technical requirements of their probation. It's a trap.

Legal scholar Michelle Alexander deftly calls this contemporary period of U.S. history "the New Jim Crow" and argues that mass incarceration is a type of modern legalized slavery, consciously created to keep Black people in the position of second-class citizens. Tens of millions of people not only have been stripped of their right to vote but have lost countless everyday freedoms as a result of being convicted of a crime. In that sense, Nixon's master plan worked. Mass incarceration is yet another dip — one that happened as a result of the progress forced into existence by the Civil Rights movement.

The final dip I'd like for you to consider brings us to a much more recent era. From 1789 until 2008, the United States elected forty-three white male presidents. I'd call that an undeniable trend, wouldn't you? But after having forty-three consecutive white male presidents over 219 consecutive years, in 2008 American voters elected a man who may very well be the most unique Black man in the entire country.

I remember first hearing about an up-and-coming political leader named Barack Hussein Obama a year after 9/11. Now his name rolls right off the tongue, but twenty years ago, not so much. The United States had never had a mainstream politician with such a name. Curious, I asked a friend, "Where's this guy from?"

"The South Side of Chicago," he replied.

Knowing that the national headquarters for the Nation of Islam were there, and that he had an African and Arabic name, I asked, "Did he used to be a member of the Nation or something?"

"Nah, man," my friend replied. "He's not actually *from* the South Side of Chicago originally. He's from Hawaii."

"Hawaii?!" I exclaimed, more confused than when we first started talking. I had never heard of a Black man being born there.

"Well," my friend continued, "his father was a scholar from Kenya and met his mother, a white woman from Kansas, while they attended college in Hawaii."

"Wow. That's different," I thought aloud.

"But get this: he actually lived a big chunk of his childhood in Indonesia," my friend added.

I was so intrigued. I had never heard such a unique origin story—and knowing that he was thinking about entering politics, I wondered if the nation would ever accept such a man. But Barack Obama first won his race for the U.S. Senate and then, taking the country by storm, beat out a host of more experienced, better-known Democrats to win the nomination for president. Next he defeated John McCain and became the forty-fourth president of the United States of America.

Almost immediately after Obama was elected, we entered into a new dip where people, particularly white men, began trying to undermine the validity of this arrangement, with some even questioning whether Barack Obama was an American citizen. It didn't matter that Obama had released his birth certificate and that his birth had been announced in Hawaii's local newspapers, and that doctors and nurses and family and friends who were present for his birth in 1961 had talked about it on the record. In this moment, facts stopped mattering in a very peculiar way. It became clear that disturbing the status quo of electing forty-three consecutive white male presidents was causing a very particular group of people to have a complete meltdown.

And the most prominent person in the nation to join in on this meltdown? Donald Trump. Over and over again, in interviews and on social media, Trump publicly questioned Obama's citizenship, even claiming to have dispatched private investigators to Hawaii to uncover the truth that Obama was not born in Hawaii and therefore was an illegitimate president. And so began Donald Trump's official entry into the world of presidential politics. Until this point in his life as a reality TV show host and frequent guest on professional wrestling pay-per-views, the notion that Trump would ever get into politics, make a serious run for president, and then win was absolutely ludicrous. But that's what happens when a game-changing innovation is introduced that disturbs the primary people in power. A dip always follows. And when a nation is in a deep dip, anything can happen.

If you think, though, that Donald Trump is the principal cause of the dip that we are currently in, then you don't understand the nature of the dip itself. Donald Trump was elected because we were already *in* one. The election of Trump just served as a catalyzing force for the white angst brewing under the surface ever since Obama took office in 2008. That said, while Trump may not have created the dip, throughout his campaign and his presidency, he has worked hard to keep us in it. He's both a symptom and a cause. And merely ousting him—or removing any single person from elected office, for that matter—will not get us out. Trump did not build the systems and structures of mass incarceration. He did not plunge this world into a climate crisis. He did not cause the epidemic of gun violence or school shootings. They existed before him and will exist after him. He and his political allies must be confronted and defeated, but this nation has systemic problems that go far beyond him.

Trump, full-fledged bigot that he is, rose to power on the back of white male insecurities. Looking back on Obama's eight years in office, his policies weren't even radical. But what *was* undeniably radical was Barack Obama's humanity — the color of his skin, the complexity of his name, the grade of his hair, his confident swagger, his preference for hip-hop, his brilliant, confident Black wife and children. Everything about Barack Obama and his family was such a steep departure from the trajectory of presidential history that his mere humanity was a disruptor.

Like so many others, I, too, was initially convinced that Obama's election was a sign that the United States was reaching new heights in an upward, progressive trajectory. Of course, I knew we weren't entering some post-racial utopia, but I foolishly thought that it meant we were at least heading in that general direction. In studying von Ranke that fateful semester in the spring of 2015, however, I came to learn that, as a human, you are either in a dip, coming out of one, or heading toward one. To assume that the dip we now find ourselves in will soon end, just on its own or after one election cycle, is to misunderstand how dips work. The human capacity for cruelty and violence is a bottomless well. This dip we now find ourselves in absolutely can worsen if we don't come together to organize our way out of it.

I wish with all my might that dips were as easy to get out of as they are to find ourselves in. But going down is always far easier than scratching and clawing your way back up. Even though societies can slowly creep into painful places of despair, the energy and effort it takes to climb out of the pit is an altogether different proposition. I am not saying here that we should plan a violent war to confront and end our greatest problems and challenges, but I am indeed saying that it will take a warlike effort of energy, planning, organization, and funding if we are to actually win this fight. It won't be won by a single hero. This new fight in front of us is going to take a movement of millions. And that includes you.

## 2

# My Story

I NEED YOU TO GO back in time with me. Before Trump.
Before Obama. Before Twitter. Before Google. Before Net-
flix. Before text messages. Way before all of that. I need you
to go back to March 8, 1995. Apartheid had just ended and
Nelson Mandela was in his first year as president of South
Africa. Tupac and Biggie were still alive and at the top of
their game. And on a random spring afternoon during my
sophomore year of high school, everything changed for me.
If getting that Facebook message about Eric Garner in July
of 2014 altered the trajectory of my adult life, then no single
moment in time impacted my young life more than what
I'm about to tell you. It almost ruined me, but had it not
happened, I am completely sure my life would've taken a
very different path. Let me take you back . . .

"Man, look at those stupid rednecks. Always messin' and shit," I said to my friend LaRon as we glanced at a fight that had broken out among the Future Farmers of America. Melees, skirmishes, squabbles, and fisticuffs were far from rare at our rural high school, the only one in our small factory and farm town of about eight thousand people, Versailles, Kentucky. Somebody always had a beef that they wanted to settle and fight through, and on this day the rural farm boys had clearly had some type of falling-out with one another.

We chuckled, half-glad that it had nothing to do with us for a change. Woodford County High School was a pressure cooker of racial violence and tension, an environment where bigotry was felt on a daily basis. Students wore Confederate flag paraphernalia; racial slurs were regularly dropped in conversation. I HATE NIGGERS was written on the bathroom stalls of our school so frequently that we didn't even report it. It was just the norm.

And while the general atmosphere of racism and bigotry was present for all Black students, I almost immediately became a target for this violence. Within the first few weeks of my freshman year, I was threatened and harassed, called a nigger and a coon, and had a jar of tobacco spit thrown directly in my face. It hadn't always been this way for me. I had been a popular bridge builder between classmates of different races and backgrounds in middle school, but Woodford County High School put the brakes on all of that quick, fast, and in a hurry.

To be exposed to this level of vitriol was shocking, to say the least. Raised by a sweet, single white woman who made lightbulbs at the local Sylvania factory, I never had "the talk" that Black families, out of sheer necessity, must give to their children about how to walk, talk, shop, drive, and breathe in a world that often deems them a threat because of the color of their skin. Even though I had been born of an interracial relationship in 1978, and had been told that I was "mixed" since I was seven years old, my mother, for all intents and purposes, raised me as racially and ethnically ambiguous. We just didn't talk about race, ever.

Growing up in my mother's house, I knew as much about the concepts of race, racism, and being biracial in the American South as I did about roofing, mechanics, or Mozart. You could say my racial IQ was only slightly higher than those of children in most white households — which is to say, it was pretty damn low. Today, at my dinner table or on an average car ride with my wife and five kids, we talk about race, racism, police brutality, injustice, Black history, Black excellence, Black Girl Magic, Black Boy Joy, hair length and texture and type and health, skin tone, Black-owned businesses, whether or not singing gospel will get Kanye an invite back to the cookout, and a thousand other quintessentially Black topics. Our kids know the stories of Sandra Bland, Tamir Rice, and Trayvon Martin as if they were related to them. They know the reasons why we hear so much about Dr. King's "I Have a Dream" speech but so little about the more radical turn his speeches took during the last six years of his life. They know that Malcolm X smiled every day and yet there is a reason why we only see pictures of him with a scowl. If I asked them what rappers' names start with K or J, Kendrick and J. Cole will come out instantly. They know the threats and odds they are up against, not just in society but out on the street or in school on an average day. And all of that's not because they are the children of an activist—this is the norm for all Black families.

Even though my understanding of racism and bigotry was limited as a child, I am so grateful for the Black families in Versailles who took me under their wing and helped me to understand my own identity. Before they started teaching me about the horrible, racist history of my hometown, I was lovingly introduced to the richness and beauty of Black culture from inside of Black homes, churches, barbershops, and family reunions. The families of Justine Laine, Monte Berry, Lionel Morton, Steven Searcy, Corey Green, Gary Carter, Teresa Brooks, Emmitt Murphy, Kim Bradshaw, and so many more welcomed me with open arms as a young boy who sometimes struggled to find his way. When Black or multiracial children grow up in white homes, the village regularly steps in to fill in the gaps.

These environments introduced me to certain foods, smells, words, jokes, tones, rhythms, moves, textures, and terms of endearment that I had never been exposed to before. At first, I felt like a welcome guest, but then, as the months and years went on, I knew that this was *me*. "Shaun, baby, you *have* to let us cut your hair. That's a white boy haircut," I remember my friend Lionel's older sister once telling me. It wasn't meant as a diss; she was looking out for me. I was twelve. "You have to put this in it," she said, showing me a small, circular orange tin can with a thick, waxy hair grease in it called Murray's Superior Hair Dressing Pomade. I used it for years before finally upgrading to Sportin' Waves. A white person has never touched my hair since.

By late elementary school and throughout junior high, I openly considered myself not mixed, not biracial, but Black, as did my peers, teachers, and counselors. Curiously, my racial identity didn't seem to matter to anyone. It just wasn't a big deal. In fact, until I reached high school, not a single thing in my life suggested that society would ever put any limits on me. I hadn't known about the violent and turbulent history of my town, the backdrop for all of the racist actions that I'd eventually confront on a daily basis. I'd later come to learn that Versailles had an ugly past, rife with both slavery and lynching. It was a tiny place, mainly composed of farmland for tobacco, but in 1850 a staggering 6,374 enslaved Africans were forced to live in Woodford County, nearly outnumbering white people. The Civil War and the abolition of slavery wrecked the economy of Versailles, which had been reliant on free, forced labor, and white people had been pissed about it ever since.

I was just fifteen years old when I got my hands on a dusty library book called *Racial Violence in Kentucky*. It was then that I first learned that during the height of Reconstruction, when African Americans were gaining power all across the country, white militias and lynch mobs targeted and killed Black folk right there in my hometown to stop their social progress. James Parker and William Turpin, two influential Black political leaders in Versailles, faced this awful fate in 1870. One August evening, Parker's home was surrounded by an angry white mob. Told that he and his family would be killed if he didn't open the door, Parker was shot to death the second he complied. The same mob then moved on to surround the home of Parker's friend William Turpin. As he attempted to escape out of a back window of his home, Turpin was shot and instantly killed. These men weren't even accused of any nonsense crimes, like whistling at white women; they were just influential and Black in a small town where those two words together weren't accepted. The murders were so horrific that the governor of Kentucky, John Stevenson, went as far as to denounce them, offering a reward and demanding that the white men who committed the crimes be held responsible. And yet nothing was done. No charges were brought. When it was clear that local officials would not protect Black people in Versailles, scores of families, both Black and white, fled the lawless town.

In the wake of these murders, other local Black leaders received letters saying that they would be next if they didn't leave town or cease organizing. And yet, even as the Black people who stayed in town kept to their own business, the violence continued. In August of 1890, a Black farmer named John Henderson was lynched on the edge of town. Decades later, in 1921, a Black man named Richard James was handed over to an angry white mob by the local jailer in Versailles and then lynched and hung from a tree, just about half a mile from my high school. As with the murders of James Parker and William Turpin, Versailles leaders refused to hold anyone accountable. It was the town's way when it came to racial injustice.

These open and public murders of Black men by angry white mobs struck deep, lasting fear into the dwindling Black community in Versailles. Dozens of prominent Black families packed up and left to move to nearby cities like Lexington, Louisville, and Cincinnati, taking their businesses with them. Those who stayed behind understood the dire consequences of even being perceived as rocking the boat. Elders in Versailles have since told me of crosses being burned in their yards, and of the ever-present threat of racial intimidation that lingered all the way through my own childhood. But as a kid, I knew none of this. I didn't realize that there was a backdrop to my town's history demanding that certain racial codes be followed or dire consequences could be faced.

When I proudly and confidently strolled into school on the first day of my freshman year, I had no idea that my identity alone would be enough to be considered problematic. Not only did I see myself as Black, but every one of my best friends was Black, my girlfriend was Black, and my white friends whom I grew up with saw me as Black. So when I arrived at high school and sat at the "Black table" in the cafeteria and continued to hang out with my Black friends, I didn't even give it a second thought. That was a problem, apparently. My very presence seemed to annoy some of the older white students at the school who did not know me or my story. In the best-case scenario, I confused them, but many racist white students, all of them complete strangers to me, were flat-out irritated that someone they perceived to be white had so flippantly broken unspoken racial codes by sitting at the Black table and chilling at the Black hangout locations around the school. It never once occurred to me that someone across the cafeteria or passing me in the hallway would look at me and wonder why I had the nerve to break convention. But in truth I wasn't breaking convention at all—I was just being myself.

Within days, older white students who looked like grown men would deliberately push me in the hallways, sometimes knocking my books out of my hands or even knocking me all the way down. A week in, all of my books were removed from my locker and thrown in trash cans throughout the school; the administration essentially shrugged when I went to complain about it. I had never been a bully or been bullied a single day in my life. I was a confident kid, but these aggressions shook me. I was equal parts embarrassed, frustrated, and mortified, and with each diss or bump or stare, I retreated into a cocoon of fear, anger, and humiliation. I was thirteen years old, one of the youngest people in the entire school, and weighed only about 115 pounds. I didn't know how to defend myself, and I didn't know whom to turn to for help.

Three weeks into my freshman year of high school, I did something simple that I honestly thought was for the greater good but that soon sent my life spiraling out of control. After the final school bell rang one day, I walked through the gymnasium toward the steel back door that I'd often exit out of as a shortcut to walk home. But before I made it there, I saw two of my childhood friends, Gary and Tim, fighting and wrestling on the gym floor. One was Black and the other was white, but this wasn't a fact that registered with me— these were just two guys I knew. A perpetual peacemaker, I walked over to them, kneeled down, and pried them off of each other. I had no idea what they were fighting over;

I didn't even care. Gary has since told me that it was just over a game of basketball. Other people rushed over to keep them separated, and I simply walked away. And that was it. *That* was the moment that changed everything. Sounds like nothing, right? I thought so as well.

For the next few days in school, white students began pointing at me in the hallways and whispering. I couldn't make sense of it; I never even considered that it had anything do with me breaking up that fight. Between classes one day, I overheard a group of rednecks, as they called themselves, loudly talking about how they were going to give me what I deserved. I knew they didn't mean it as a compliment, but I was too green to really understand what they meant. That Friday, I found out.

By the time I reached high school, I had played trumpet for four years, spending the summer before freshman year going to daily practices for the high school marching band in the humid Kentucky weather. In our sleepy little town, home football games were a huge deal. The opening home game of the season was a special event, and it would be the first time our marching band would get to perform our newly choreographed halftime show for a live audience. My dear brother Jason, who passed away while I was writing this book, was in the marching band for all four years of high school. He had graduated and gone off to college, but he came back home that weekend to see my performance.

We nailed the halftime performance, and I was feeling good. After the show, the lead band instructor, Nathanael Carter, who was the only African American teacher in the entire high school who didn't also coach sports, gave us the third quarter off to hang with friends and get some refreshments before we were expected to return to the stands to play during the fourth quarter. A few of us were walking together to get some snacks when a hillbilly named Blake walked up to us and said, in a very jovial and friendly manner, that a few guys "wanted to talk" with me.

Naive as ever, I was legitimately curious as to who wanted to speak with me. Dressed in our full marching band regalia, my friends and I followed Blake past the refreshment stand, past the restrooms, past the PTA volunteer booth, and down a hill into a field, where about twenty white students were waiting. It was a setup. As they surrounded me in a tight circle, fear leapt into my throat. I wondered for a moment if I was going to die on that field. My friends, seeing how much trouble I was in, ran for their lives to get help.

Suddenly Tim, the white student I had separated from the fight the week prior, emerged from the crowd. Tim had been my friend since elementary school, when we lived just five houses away from each other on McDonald Drive. He had spent the night at my house on many occasions, when we'd play the classic football game *Tecmo Bowl,* making the rule that neither of us was allowed to choose the Raiders because Bo Jackson just could not be stopped. As the young men began yelling at Tim to hit me, my feelings were crushed. I tried to explain to Tim that I didn't want to fight him, that I had no problem whatsoever with him, and that we didn't need to do this. I meant every word, but I also wanted to stall until somebody, anybody, arrived to rescue me. When it became clear that there was not going to be any defusing this situation, I took off my fancy band uniform jacket so that it wouldn't get ruined in whatever happened next.

After what seemed like a lifetime but in reality was only a few minutes, my friends returned with what appeared to be at least twenty Black students, graduates, and family members. A sense of relief overcame me. I had been so nervous that I felt like I might pass out. *At least I'm not going to die,* I thought to myself. With my whole crew there to back me up, I did not intend to fight, but several white students suddenly pushed me into Tim, and the fighting began. We pummeled each other, first standing up, then rolling around on the ground. And the next thing I knew, it was as if a bear had picked me up and carried me away.

My brother Jason was the perfect citizen and one of the most reliable, consistent human beings I have ever known. We both grew up without our fathers, but in his local Boy Scout troop, several genuinely good men took Jason under their wing. And one of his mentors was a big, burly, bearded man named Mr. John Lodmell. People called him Big John. His son, also named John, was one of my brother's best friends and a fellow Eagle Scout. I didn't really know either John personally, but when word spread throughout the stadium that I had been surrounded by that group of white students, Mr. Lodmell, presumably out of love for my brother, made his way down that steep hill, waded into the crowd, grabbed me like a sack of potatoes, and carried me back up to the stadium, where he told me to wait until my brother came to get me. Still stunned from the punches I'd absorbed and the stress of the whole situation, I could hardly believe what I was experiencing. Jason soon arrived, rushing me to his car and then speeding me home to safety.

After I left with my brother, three more large brawls broke out between Black and white students in what ended up being the largest racial altercation ever at Woodford County High School. I didn't even know those fights had happened until my friends called me the next day. When I showed up at school the following Monday, I was immediately summoned to the front office. Without allowing me to say so much as a word in my own defense, the assistant principal informed me that I had been suspended from school for fighting, and I should not return until Thursday. I had never been in any real trouble until that moment, and now I was being punished for a fight I didn't even want to be in. It was deeply upsetting and confusing.

During the three days I was forced to stay home from school, racial tensions boiled over. Unbeknownst to me, in the fights following the one I was in, racial slurs had been used, and white students wearing Confederate flag T-shirts and bandannas had gotten involved. With the racial powder keg fully sparked, administrators at the school were struggling to keep everything together. To try to mitigate the tension, the school determined that it was going to ban all students from wearing Confederate flags. White students fought back with the retort that if they couldn't wear Confederate flags, Black students couldn't wear Malcolm X T-shirts or paraphernalia, which were still super popular following the release of the Spike Lee movie two years earlier. They then staged a walkout over the schoolwide ban of Confederate imagery, an event that was widely covered by the regional television news outlets and even newspapers in Lexington.

When I returned from that suspension, with Confederate flags now completely banned from the school, it was as if I had written the edict to remove them myself. The anger and abuse that I had experienced on a daily basis during my first few weeks of high school instantly went from casual to severe. Every day in school was a nightmare. I was afraid to walk down the halls alone and would get nauseous every time the bell rang for class to end. While I would only catch a few stares in class, my safety was guaranteed as long as I was in the presence of a teacher. As soon as I crossed the threshold of the classroom into the hallways, I was in my own personal hell. Sometimes the rednecks would be waiting for me as I made my way from one class to another. One day, as I left algebra class, an older white student and two of his friends surrounded me. I was grabbed by my shirt and lifted off the ground before being slammed into a locker like a rag doll. My body and soul crumpled; I was so afraid of what was going to happen next that I remember for the first time in my life wishing I was dead.

Luckily, in this case, I was able to get out of the situation with the help of an older Black student named Eric Bradley, a celebrated artist in the school who had painted several murals in the halls. Eric and I weren't close friends, but he was the cousin of one of my best friends, Lionel. Lionel and Eric's entire family was like a surrogate family to me. His dear mother, whom we all called Mrs. Betty, was one of the gentlest and kindest women I had ever met in my life. She treated me like her son, and Lionel's extended family was equally as kind. I had never heard Eric do so much as raise his voice in my entire life; I didn't even know he could get angry. When my defeated eyes met his in that hallway, I would've understood if he saw who was about to kick my ass and decided to keep walking. Instead, he demanded that they let me go, roaring in between the three of them and shoving them aside before picking me up and carrying me about twenty feet down the hallway. *"Run,"* he told me. We never spoke of it again.

With no father or father figure to speak of, and my big brother away at college, I felt the full burden and stress of protecting myself. My mother had proudly just bought her first home — across the street from the high school, so that I could get back and forth easily — but the reality was that the environment around Versailles was no longer safe for me. This became glaringly apparent after I decided to walk home alone after a school dance the fall of freshman year. It was like something out of a 1980s horror movie. Unbeknownst to me, a pickup truck full of rednecks was waiting for me outside of the dance, idling with its lights off. As I began walking down the long, dark driveway behind the school, the pickup's headlights flashed as it slowly began inching toward me. Immediately, my fear spiked; I was a sitting duck, trapped between the school on the left and a fence on the right. As I started picking up my pace, the students starting yelling and laughing from the windows. Suddenly the driver stepped on the gas and the truck came barreling in my direction. I ran like hell, completely convinced that they were about to run me over. Within seconds, the truck was nearly at my heels, forcing me to jump onto the fence to keep from getting killed. Instead of driving on, as I had hoped they would, they stopped the truck and began yelling at me through the rolled-down window. Clinging to the fence, I glanced back, recognizing at least two of the young men. They seemed to be having such a great time at my expense. I had no idea how I'd get home and didn't feel remotely safe making the walk alone. I shuffled my sweaty, terrified self back to the dance, but all of my friends had already left. After a few minutes, I peeked my head out the back door to see if the truck was gone. It was. And I made another one of many dangerous walks home.

I rarely told my mother about the abuse I suffered, wanting to protect her from the cruelty, but this incident was different. When I got home from the dance, I had to fight to hold back tears, but I eventually broke down and told her what had happened. She was equal parts crushed and livid. I told her that I had already reported multiple incidents before this one to the administration and that the school had done nothing to protect me. She had an idea. This time, she wanted me to record myself reporting the incident to the school principals, to get a full account of their reaction. She purchased a tiny microcassette recorder from our local RadioShack and told me to keep it in my pocket. And I did just that. Again the school took my report, called the students into the office while I was there, and, as punishment, merely asked them to apologize. I recorded every bit of their insincere pledges, my heart sinking. Slowly but surely, white students were being taught that they could cause me any harm they wanted without serious repercussions. The word was out.

As a coping mechanism for this trauma, I started chronically skipping school, forging notes from my mother. It was a pretty easy hustle — she left for work before I woke up and didn't get home from the factory until after school was over. I stayed home watching movies, making mixtapes, eating Pizza Rolls, and dreaming about moving out of Versailles one day. My grades tanked, but each day I skipped meant one more day I could avoid the abuse. It also meant feeling lonely and isolated for the first time in my life. For years, I had been popular, a social butterfly, thriving off of people laughing at my jokes or wanting my advice, but now I was becoming a hermit, sinking into depression. It was in that space, at that time, that I first learned to wear a mask and flash a fake smile to hide my brokenness.

I did just enough to pass all of my classes my freshman year and used the summer to work, make some money, date every girl I liked even a little bit, and simply recover from it all. Between the fall of freshman year and the fall of sophomore year, I grew six inches, put on nearly twenty-five pounds, and became a little more confident about how to defend myself if I had to. By the time I made it to March of my sophomore year, I was a grizzled veteran, an expert at avoiding the abuse. While I still had incidents here and there, several of my biggest tormentors had graduated, so I sincerely thought the worst was behind me. I never accounted for the possibility of what I was about to experience that spring day.

My homie LaRon and I were in a good mood that fateful Wednesday afternoon. The hardest part of our school day was over, and we were shooting the shit and chilling out at the Black hangout spot before I had to head to band class. Of course, there was no COLORED ONLY sign for us at this spot, but like clockwork—before school started, between classes, and after the final school bell rang—if you had a drop of melanin, you hung out in the corner by the entrance to the gymnasium. It wasn't special, but, dammit, it was ours. This was where we lovingly cracked jokes on one another, talked about which girls had the biggest booty, and argued over whether East Coast or West Coast hip-hop was better. For all I knew, the little spot by the gym had been the Black hangout spot for decades.

If I didn't stop, the walk from our hangout spot to my band class normally took only about thirty seconds. If I busted a fast jog, I could do it in less. Had I known that I was about to meet my maker, I would've brought LaRon with me on that short journey. He was a big dude, barrel-chested, a linebacker, also jolly as could be, but somebody only a fool would cross. Me, on the other hand, in spite of my growth spurt, I was still smaller than Allen Iverson. I was scrappy and fit, but those two qualities didn't strike fear in anybody.

When I turned around to give LaRon a dap and told him that I'd see him later, I had no reason to second-guess myself. I had made that brisk walk from the gym to band class hundreds of times across the previous three and a half semesters, and those treks were consistently uneventful. This was my safe hallway. I could think of ten different places in the school that felt dangerous to me, but that path was simply not one of them. My guard was all the way down, even though there was a rowdy group of rednecks fighting ahead.

As I got closer to the group of about fifteen or twenty people, something peculiar happened. The crowd, which had just been unruly enough for LaRon and me to comment on a few minutes before, grew eerily silent. It was unnerving, but I didn't know what to make of it as I walked to move past them. Suddenly I heard one voice say, "That's him," and another say, "Yeah, that's Shaun King," before a third voice yelled, "Go!"

That crowd that LaRon and I had chuckled about wasn't there because they were fighting one another. They were there for me.

In seconds, I was surrounded on every side by a group of bloodthirsty country boys, without a friend in sight or a teacher to intervene. Before I had time to thoughtfully consider an exit, I felt a wallop against the back of my head, as if I'd been hit with a baseball bat. Strangely, I felt no pain. While the blow did not knock me out, it knocked every bit of intelligence out of me.

Like most boys in the nineties, I had watched every Jean-Claude Van Damme and Steven Seagal movie ever made up until that point. VHS tapes of *Lionheart* and *Hard to Kill* were in heavy rotation on the thirteen-inch TV/VCR combo my mother had allowed me to keep in my tiny bedroom. I would watch those movies alone and reenact the fight scenes with regularity, even making the clumsy noises along with Jean-Claude when I would kick the crap out of my invisible enemies. On this day, not a single lesson my martial arts heroes had taught me mattered one bit.

Soon I felt blows hitting my face and stomach and ribs and back from every angle. I could hear the thuds of fists against my flesh and bones. My glasses went flying off my face; I was blind without them. I didn't tell my body to crumple, but it seemed like I was no longer in charge of what it did from that point forward. I instinctively curled up into the fetal position and tried to cover my face as steel-toed work boots punted and stomped and pounded my body. It seemed as if time had slowed to a snail's pace, and my mind began drifting somewhere strange. Blow after blow continued to rain down on me, but I was growing numb and distant from it all. I knew something terrible was happening, but I soon found myself not even caring about it. Darkness began enveloping my mind. Drifting out of consciousness, I heard a girl screaming at the top of her lungs. Days later I learned it was my good friend Joyce, who realized that it was me on the ground getting mauled.

Joyce's screams caused enough of a commotion to attract teachers to the scene. When students told Mr. Carter, our band director, that it was me on the ground, he, too, entered the fray to help break it up. He made sure Joyce and other band students who were caught up in the melee all went safely back to class. As teachers and staff swarmed in and intervened, every student who'd punched and kicked me fled, mainly to a wing of the school that I had never once ventured into, designed just for agriculture studies.

Amid the chaos, I was somehow left alone on the floor, bleeding, beaten, and barely conscious. I struggled to get on my feet and began shuffling toward the front office before eventually collapsing against some lockers. It sounds silly now, but I remember feeling crushed that blood covered my brand-new tennis shoes. Money was hard to come by in our house, and I'd typically only get one new pair of shoes per year.

I could not will myself to get up, no matter how hard I tried. Thankfully, one of my best friends, Rico, a pudgy, comedic brother who doubled as my barber, found me there, mumbling incoherently to myself. He helped me up and virtually carried me down two long hallways to the administrative offices at the front entrance to the school. Once we made it there, I literally collapsed right in the middle of the lobby before they dragged me into an office.

There, Mrs. Jean Whiteman, a gentle soul who was the head of the gifted-and-talented program at the school, and perhaps the only teacher I'd had up to that point who consistently gave a damn about my future, consoled me and held my hand. Ms. McGarrity, the young cheerleading coach who doubled as a computer and typing instructor, knelt beside me as well. Beyond being severely injured, I was in full-on shock and was struggling to fully comprehend the gravity of the situation. I asked the teachers to call my mother and tell her what had happened. In that moment, she was the only person I truly trusted. I knew it would create a panic, and that she would have to be pulled off the factory floor to take the call, but I didn't know what else to do. Upon hearing the news, my mom got in her white Dodge Neon and hauled ass to the school. When she arrived, she was furious at how she had been able to get this message, find someone to take her place on the floor, clock out, and drive clear across town before either the police or an ambulance showed up. We later learned that the school had called neither. She decided to rush me to the hospital herself.

In the car, the biological defenses that had allowed me to be exceedingly pummeled without ever quite feeling the specific pain of the assault began to wear off. Agonizing jolts came rushing to my nose, teeth, cheeks, and eyes, the back of my head, my ribs, legs, and, most critically, my upper and lower back. At that point in my young life, it was the worst pain I had ever felt; every tiny little movement I'd make, every bump we hit in the road, was overwhelming. Over the next few days, I would undergo a battery of tests that confirmed the severity of the situation. Doctors told me that I had a concussion, fractures to my face and ribs, badly damaged sinuses, and severely damaged discs in my lower back.

After my mother had arrived at the school and taken me to the hospital, the principal finally broke down and called the police. Detective Keith Broughton was assigned to the case, and he made his way to the hospital to meet my mother and me. To him, this was super routine: a short conversation, a blip on the radar. The whole thing took less than two minutes. When he'd completed his report and was doing a cursory check-through, he did two things that would come back to haunt me years later as a public-facing activist: he checked one box saying that I was white and another box saying he observed only minor injuries.

In the twenty years after I was assaulted, I had never once seen or read his police report, but as I began fighting for justice against police brutality, the conservative smut outlet Breitbart and one of its lead writers, Milo Yiannopoulos—who has since been banned from social media—released it as if it were some kind of smoking gun proving that I was secretly white. People even questioned whether I had been assaulted at all or had sustained the injuries that changed my entire life. Speaking to reporters in 2015, Broughton clarified what had happened that day. "I believe that he's biracial. I could just tell when I saw him. I marked him white because he's very light-complected. He was there with his white mother. On my crime report there's only two things you can check: black or white. It doesn't say biracial . . . anyone from around here who knew him knew he was mixed."

The injuries I received that day, to my body and to my soul, deeply changed who I was and who I would become. By the time I got home from the hospital, I could hardly move. In a few days, my entire back was black-and-blue from being kicked and stomped. Yet, on my first night home, white men in a pickup truck drove into the middle of my mother's front yard and began peeling out, sending grass and mud everywhere. A brave neighbor across the street named Joshua Hale, whose father was the pastor of a small Black church in town, came running out of his house, armed with nothing more than a large flashlight and a loud voice to scare them off. Luckily, it was enough to finally get them to leave our yard. My mother and I were terrified.

The following two years were without a doubt some of the most difficult of my life. The previous two had been full of racist taunts and attacks, but what was ahead was a solitary struggle. Whatever I thought I knew about myself, my life, my limits, my hopes, my dreams, my past, and my future was set ablaze on that brutal day in that high school hallway. My life as I knew it was over. I missed most of the next two years of high school recovering from multiple spinal surgeries. The recovery from those surgeries and the unending sessions of physical therapy were nearly as traumatic as the assault itself. Later, a wonderful and compassionate psychiatrist diagnosed me with PTSD. I was broken—both inside and out. I wish I could say that it didn't destroy me, but it did—just not irreparably. From that day forward, I had to truly be rebuilt—part by part, piece by piece.

By the time I emerged from surgeries and rehab and therapy, it was clear that I would likely live in physical pain for the rest of my life, and that I was going to have to somehow learn to embrace my pain, learn from it, and sever all ties with the temptation to become a bitter victim or a violent victimizer, as so many people who suffer abuse often tragically become. And yet, I did try and seek justice for these actions. My mother and I filed a lawsuit against my high school, the staff, and the county school district for their many failures that ultimately led to my assault. For nearly two years, we were determined to hold the school and the county accountable for their actions, a painful process that involved dredging up memories and opening up wounds even as they were still healing. When I finally left Versailles to attend Morehouse College, in Atlanta, I made the difficult decision to drop the suit. As much as I would've liked to have gotten some legal validation of the injuries I sustained, both physically and mentally, I needed a fresh start, and the lawsuit effectively kept my heart and soul centered in the pain of my past when I needed to move on. It was in that moment, as a seventeen-year-old freshman at Morehouse, that I promised my dear mother I would fight for justice from then on.

I didn't share this story with you to try and win your sympathy, but so that you would see how essential my own personal story is to the work I do today fighting for victims of violence and standing up against white supremacy and bigotry. I didn't know it then, but a deep sense of justice was being branded onto my soul as I experienced all of that hate. None of it seemed to have any point or redemptive value at the time, but it ultimately created a real sensitivity in me toward people who experience injustice and people who are in pain, both physical and mental. I am certainly not glad that I went through all that I went through as a young man, but I am sure that, had I not endured it, my path in life would've been different.

Your own personal story is going to fuel and inform some of the very important decisions I am about to ask you to make. Your path to change will eventually intersect with many people and causes, but right now it begins with you and you alone. The ball is completely in your court. And here's the beautiful news: every single thing you need to get started in your quest to change the world, you have right now. You, yourself, are enough. Your story has brought you this far, and now it's time for you to decide what's next. Let's dig in.

*Part Two*

# What You Must Do

WHEN WE ARE BORN into this world, we are placed into circumstances that are beyond our control. We don't choose our families or the society that raises us or the systems of oppression that we encounter based on our mere humanity alone. So much of that was determined long before we were born. But the future is not set in stone. The greatest gift to us is that we get to shape it. That awesome opportunity is available to all, no matter your background or your socioeconomic level or your race or identity. That's why it's urgent that you make a clear choice to use your life, your influence, and your resources to make this world a much better place. You have more power and potential than I think you truly understand. Part two is all about how you can position yourself to use that power.

In the previous chapter, I told you my story; now

it's time to talk about yours. Making change starts with one huge decision, a decision that comes from a place of deep personal contemplation. This decision not only will change the course of your life, but it will affect the cause you care about the most. In the next chapter, I will share more of my journey and how I chose to make my commitment to a cause. I'll also give you some guidelines on how you can identify yours. In chapter 4, I'll directly confront the greatest enemies of change and help you to overcome them. In chapter 5, I will have a frank, practical talk with you about what the first steps to making change are going to look and feel like — and trust me, it can get a little uncomfortable. And in chapter 6, I want you to begin considering what it will mean for you to use your greatest gifts and passions to make the world a better place.

3

# To Make Change, You Must First Make a Choice

THIS CHAPTER IS NOT just about your story; it's about your deciding what is going to come next in your life. It's about living intentionally, guided by hopes and goals and decisions, instead of allowing the actions of other people and corporations to drag you along every day. You need to have that type of personal clarity in order to make specific choices about your role as a change agent in this world. We are in a steep, frightening, sometimes overwhelming dip in history, and we will not get out of it without the battle of our lives. Victory will come only as a result of thoughtful consideration of how your own experiences can be channeled into good for the whole. My decision to focus on the changes I wanted to fight for in the world emerged directly from my own personal story — and yours will, too.

Deep inside each of us is a longing to do good and make a difference in the world. But what I've come to learn is that until you make a serious decision about where you're going to dedicate your time, skills, energy, and resources, your efficacy as a changemaker will be limited. Change—I mean real, systemic, lasting change—is *never* accidental. It emanates first from an individual's personal decision to stare down a problem in the world and recognize that they will be one of the people out there working to confront it. That takes guts. It takes character. And that action emerges from a deeply personal place. Later in this chapter, I'm going to guide you through the decision-making process that will put you on a focused lifelong path to systemic change. It's going to take some reflecting. It might be difficult. But I promise you it will be worth it. To help you see how to get there in your own life, I'm going to share more of my story.

Just as Leopold von Ranke sought to lay out all of history on a timeline to see if it would help him understand trends in human behavior, I did the same for my own life. And what I found was that the extreme nature of some of the most formative years of my life ultimately changed the very path that I was on.

Versailles, Kentucky, was my own personal hell during my high school years. As I recovered from my spinal surgeries, a tutor brought me my homework and sat alongside me in my bed or on the couch as I worked through my assignments. It took everything I had to graduate on time. Each class, each grade, each task put me closer to escaping the place that had nearly pulled me under. I was obsessed with getting out. My mother was also determined to see to it that

I would leave central Kentucky and never look back. Education was the key to that. After traveling to Atlanta on three separate occasions as a high school senior, I realized that Morehouse College was the place for me. In fact, it was literally the only college I applied to—something I'd *never* let my own kids do, now that I look back on it. I had no backup plans. I just knew intuitively that I was meant to be there. And when I got in, it was the first time in my life that I felt like I was fulfilling my destiny.

Morehouse represented a fresh start for me. No bullies. No rednecks. No pickup trucks. No white supremacy. It was a beautiful, peaceful mecca of Black manhood with nearly three thousand proud young Black men attending from thirty-eight states and nearly twenty countries. At Morehouse, Black people ran everything—from the security to the landscaping to the dorms to the cafeteria to the classrooms and the boardrooms. It was like our own personal Wakanda. There, we felt like we could safely let our guard down and just be curious young Black men. The swagger and masks that we would often feel pressured to wear in society weren't necessary there. Police brutality and racism didn't even exist in that beautiful bubble. We actually loved our campus police officers—an all-Black police force that knew us by name and were only there to protect us and to keep outsiders from entering the campus to cause us any harm. And so it was there, on that campus, in perfect peace, that I started to rebuild my confidence, letting go of the hurt of the past. In high school, every single day was hard. There, I had been focused more on survival than on my own growth and development. Morehouse was the exact opposite. It ended up being an incubator, not just for me but for so many of us who had grown up in dangerous circumstances where we were denied a fair chance to learn or lead.

My major was African American studies, which was a rather new program inside of the history department. There I found my people, like-minded students who were equally frustrated about systemic racism and injustice and were determined to do something about it. I had never had a single Black teacher my entire life until I got to Morehouse. Most of us hadn't. Now we were being taught revolutionary new paradigms about manhood and masculinity, power, leadership, and social change, by men like Professors Larry Crawford and Kurt Young, as well as Drs. Aaron Parker, Marcellus Barksdale, and Melvin Rahming. I learned more about myself and my place in the world during the first semester of my freshman year than I had learned in my whole life up to that point. And I thrived in this new environment. Right out of the gate, I became president of my dorm, a volunteer in King Chapel, and an active presence in a vibrant, African-centered Black Consciousness community that had formed at the Atlanta University Center.

It would be hard to fully explain just how radical I was during this time, but let me try to paint a picture for you. When I was later sworn in as student government president, I wore a dashiki and raised a Black Power fist in the air the whole time. I owned my own megaphone and had a backup battery pack for it. I was *that* guy. I was Captain Woke! (To be clear, I mean that in the cheesiest way possible.)

And it just so happened that I was *that* guy at Morehouse during a time when students were really looking for *that* guy. We came of age during the height of the so-called war on drugs. James Byrd Jr. was lynched by white supremacists in Texas the summer after my freshman year. George W. Bush was elected president, 9/11 happened, and the war in Afghanistan began all while I was a student. At Morehouse, the average brother had a super-high political IQ and was hyper-informed in a way that was invigorating. We weren't just a group of teenagers who wanted better food options in the cafeteria (although we desperately needed that); we wanted a more Afrocentric curriculum and were concerned about gentrification happening around our campus. Together we fought against the disparities in sentencing for crack versus powder cocaine, and we worked hard to free Kemba Smith, a Hampton University student who had been sentenced to twenty-four years in prison for a first-time drug offense when she was caught with drugs in the car belonging to her abusive boyfriend. Fighting for people and causes gave me a deep sense of purpose and allowed me to take my mind off my past and channel my energy into helping other people in need.

During this time, I was lucky enough to get a work-study job as the student assistant for Dr. Marcellus Barksdale, who was not only the director of African American studies but a brilliant mentor to so many of us. His cozy, book-lined office on the third floor of Brawley Hall became the unofficial hangout spot for me and my crew. It was there, in that office, that I first heard the name Amadou Diallo.

I remember that moment so clearly. My friend Harold, a

tall, thin, jet-Black brother from Milwaukee and probably the only student I knew on campus who was more serious than I was, asked us if we had heard the story of Amadou Diallo. I shook my head. "Never heard of him," I replied. You have to understand that this was before cell phones had web browsers and news apps. The internet was still in its infancy. Our dorm rooms didn't have cable television, so we watched very little news. It had taken nearly ten days for word of Amadou's murder to reach our tiny, sacred space in southwest Atlanta.

"NYPD shot this brother forty-one times," Harold said, taking that seriousness of his up a notch. "Can you believe that shit?"

"Forty-one?" I asked, my mind still catching up to the number. I thought maybe I had heard him wrong.

"Yeah, they fired forty-one shots at this man and killed him right on the doorstep of his home," Harold replied.

He went on to explain that four white police officers—Edward McMellon, Sean Carroll, Kenneth Boss, and Richard Murphy—had killed this young, gentle soul who had immigrated to the United States with his mother from Guinea to pursue more opportunities. They came for the American Dream and instead experienced an unthinkable nightmare. A silence fell over the room as we struggled to process such brutality. Hearing the news shook me to my core. Across the country, other college students just like us were learning of his murder in their own very analog ways. It was our Ferguson moment a full generation before the murder of Michael Brown. Amadou Diallo became the first name of a Black man murdered by police in the United

States that I memorized and enshrined in what would eventually become a full catalog of hundreds of such names in my mind.

In so many ways, Morehouse was like a refuge for us, a place where we were valued and protected from all the threats and dangers of society. But the murder of Amadou Diallo that year caused us to see ourselves as citizens of a much bigger world. Hundreds of Morehouse students were from New York and had directly experienced the brutality and bigotry of the NYPD, and several asked me to use my influence and platform as a student leader and activist on and around campus to speak out about the murder of Amadou. And I did mention him, every chance I got, in front of crowds large and small. The student body was both energized and outraged. That winter, a group of us joined other campus-based NAACP chapters and traveled to New York to protest, marching alongside thousands of others from around the country who were demanding justice. It was so damn cold that we could hardly stand it, and we mainly felt like we were clumsily joining somebody else's work in progress, but the moment of solidarity with strangers from all around the country moved each of us deeply. When we got back to Morehouse, we continued our mission, writing letters and emails to politicians asking them to stand up for Amadou, and spreading the word to anybody and everybody we could about the case. These efforts went on for a full year, not just on our campus but all over the country. We were proud that we were participating in the conversation, and it sparked something in me, in that I learned how I could connect my studies and my student leadership experience with the powerful act of speaking truth to power and fighting for justice.

As the trial approached and the calls for justice grew louder, my friends and I didn't know what I know now about the inner workings of the justice system. It felt as if the legal system in New York had rigged the case to ensure that the NYPD officers would never be held accountable. The trial was moved out of New York City and 150 miles upstate to Albany — far away from a jury that may have been more willing to convict the officers. And on February 25, 2000, the officers who shot and killed Amadou were found not guilty on all charges.

I was crushed. I had fully believed that our efforts, alongside the efforts of organizers and activists in New York and all across the country, were going to make a real difference. We had all assumed that the nation had progressed to a place where justice for the Diallo family would be possible in a way that had never been afforded the family of Emmett Till and countless others before him. To get that verdict was a gut punch, and a deeply instructive moment. Amadou had been young, just twenty-three years old. He was our peer. It reminded us that the systems that we were pleading with for justice were never designed to give such a thing to Black people. On the contrary, they were designed for the enslavement and punishment of Black folk. When I arrived at Morehouse, I had been through hell and high water, but I don't know that I had an authentic worldview yet. It left my blood boiling and caused me to begin considering how I could somehow tilt my life toward helping families like Amadou's to get the justice they deserved.

Soon thereafter, one by one, our close crew began to graduate from Morehouse. I never wanted to leave that place. Many of my deepest wounds had started to heal during my time there, and for this small window of my life, for the very first time, I had been able to fully let my guard down. I mattered. My humanity mattered. My voice mattered. My plans and protests mattered. And the thought of leaving that cocoon made me nervous. The rules at Morehouse were created for our success. Outside of Morehouse, it wasn't just that the rules were changed. The game itself was completely different.

After graduation, I received several corporate job offers and even considered pursuing a few of them. I had gotten married to my high school sweetheart, Rai, and we welcomed our first child into the world. We got our first apartment together, a few blocks from Atlanta's Six Flags amusement park; the rent was only around $700 a month, but we still struggled to pay it sometimes. A well-paid corporate consulting job with Bain or Boston Consulting Group seemed like a way to solve a lot of our problems, but I just didn't have it in me. I knew that whatever career I was going to pursue after graduating, it would have to be focused on helping people. I packed my megaphone away in a closet, became a schoolteacher, and began pouring all of my energy into providing for my sweet young family. My heart for racial justice didn't die, but the huge shifts in my life essentially ended my public activism. After all of my classmates graduated and relocated all over the country and around the world, I lacked an organizing community to be a part of to do the work.

It was a full thirteen years later when I received that Facebook message from a former classmate of mine informing me of the public lynching of Eric Garner. For virtually every day of those thirteen years in between, I aimed to help people: I taught middle and high school history and civics; I worked for years as a full-time teacher and counselor in Atlanta's youth detention centers; I was a counselor at a residential hospital for severely abused children; I was a pastor at a church in midtown Atlanta; I traveled the country as a motivational speaker; I started a crowdfunding platform called HopeMob, designed to provide tangible support to people in crisis. But over and over again, my life kept bringing me back to the cause of justice. I had advocated for Sean Bell when the NYPD shot him fifty times on his wedding day in 2006. Later that year, I spoke out on behalf of six young Black boys who had been jailed in Louisiana, known as the Jena Six. I organized, advocated, and fundraised for justice for Trayvon Martin when he was stalked and murdered by a violent bigot in his own neighborhood. But it was that Facebook message I received about Eric Garner—and the subsequent murders of Michael Brown, John Crawford III, and Ezell Ford over the next three weeks —that truly awakened something in me, and reminded me of who I had once pledged to be when I dropped my own case against those who had victimized me as a child.

In 2014, at the age of thirty-four, with all of the energy I could muster, I made the decision to focus my whole life on fighting mass incarceration and police brutality. And when I made this decision, it was as though everything in my world aligned. It clicked. I don't mean that the work got easy—it was and remains brutally difficult—but I'm saying that it felt *right*. People who had known me my whole adult life reached out to say, "This is who we always knew you would be," and I understand exactly why they said that. I don't regret taking thirteen years of my adult life getting to that decision, because I learned so much along the way, but when I made it, I knew I was walking in my purpose.

I didn't know exactly where this path would take me. I didn't know how I would provide for my family. I didn't know what it meant to be an effective organizer. I didn't know who my friends and allies would be. I didn't know what the opposition I was going to face would look or feel like. But I made a decision to throw my entire life into fighting against police brutality and mass incarceration—not just because the moment called for it, but because doing so was the natural progression of my entire life.

I'm telling you this because I need you to reflect on your own path and journey, and I need you to make a difficult, painful decision. I need you to think about one single problem in the world that bothers you more than anything—the cause that breaks your heart, makes you to lose sleep, has brought tears to your eyes or anger to your bones. What one problem in the world disturbs you *so much* that you'd do almost anything to solve it? I'm talking about something that has bothered you for years, something your brain has developed a radar for. Maybe you've posted about it on social media or you bring the issue up in conversations and talk to people about it. Or maybe it's so painful you haven't been able to do that. This is the issue that resonates most with your soul. I'd like for you to take a few moments to reflect back over your life and consider the causes and problems in the world that you have been consistently frustrated and concerned about.

I am asking you to decide to make *that* problem into *your* problem. As much as you would care about a water pipe that burst above your bedroom, I want you to determine within yourself that you are going to tilt your whole life to solving this particular problem in the world. Because what I have learned is that complex systemic problems get solved only by people who make hardcore decisions to solve them. Period. Full stop. And you don't have to be fully confident about where to start once you make that decision, either. Are you a plumber? Probably not. But I bet if that pipe burst over your bedroom, you'd shift furniture, make calls, get buckets, search Google and Yelp, and move heaven and earth to get that problem solved. We solve problems that we're determined to solve. I need you to get determined to solve just one single serious problem in the world, dammit!

It's important to remember not to base this decision on fads or trends. The popularity and momentum of causes comes and goes; trending topics shouldn't determine your choice. And you shouldn't necessarily commit to the same cause that people you admire are committed to, either. When you make a decision to fight back against an evil or ill in this world, it needs to come from your heart, your gut, your instincts. This issue must come out of *your* life experience. It must be so deeply connected to the way you feel, on a cellular level, that you will dedicate the rest of your life to fight for it. That is the level of long-term dedication that is necessary to make change.

Making this decision is not easy. At first, choosing just one problem to solve when there are so many things wrong with the world is going to feel like it violates your spirit, but I swear to you, it's necessary. To decide that you are going to focus the bulk of your time, energy, and resources on solving one problem requires you to admit that you aren't a superhero. You don't have unlimited powers or unlimited time. You aren't an eccentric billionaire with an unlimited budget. You are a finite being with very practical limitations. And while you can care deeply about many issues or be affected by several issues in very tangible ways, attempting to fight for breakthrough change on more than one problem drastically decreases the likelihood that you'll be effective in solving any of them. But when you make an issue your specialty, your obsession, and the primary recipient of your creative energy, you are more likely to actually have an impact on it.

And know this now: the thing that breaks your heart may not even matter that much to other people. In fact, if I asked an audience of one hundred people, "What is the one thing that keeps you up at night?" I'd get seventy-five different answers. We often operate under the inaccurate assumption that what matters most to us is the same for everybody else, but the thing that breaks your heart may not resonate so deeply with others in your life. And that's okay.

Out of ignorance and immaturity, I used to think that *your* cause of choice needed to match my cause, because my cause is the *real* problem that must be addressed right here and now. To this day, I see that type of thinking among activists and organizers all around the world. And I understand why. To force your agenda and cause into the mainstream, to force solutions and policies onto legislative calendars and corporate budgets, to build grassroots momentum, you have to act with such a fierce, singular urgency that you can fully convince yourself that your cause matters more than every other cause in the universe. But those fighting mass incarceration can't knock those fighting the climate crisis, just as those fighting for voting rights can't knock those fighting for women's rights or educational access or animal rights. All of these fights are essential. Our world has so many pressing needs that any single person is ill-equipped to fight all of them. But the most critical thing is this: you cannot allow yourself to be so overwhelmed by the sheer volume of problems in our world that the stress of it all causes you to be noncommittal about helping solve any of them. Doing that makes you no more effective than the politicians offering "thoughts and prayers" and nothing else after every school shooting. And I know that's not who you want to be.

A few years ago, I spoke at Bates College, in Lewiston, Maine, the alma mater of one of my lifelong heroes, Dr. Benjamin Elijah Mays. Dr. Mays graduated from Bates in 1920, at a time when few African Americans had even set foot in the state of Maine. He later became the president of Morehouse College for twenty-seven of its strongest, most courageous years. Dr. King called Mays "my spiritual mentor and my intellectual father." Indeed, it was Mays who gave both the benediction after King's famous "I Have a Dream" speech and his eulogy after King was assassinated. Walking around that campus, knowing that Dr. Mays once traversed those same grounds as a young man, was a special experience. I could not imagine how far from home he must've felt. Both of his parents had been born into slavery, on plantations in Virginia and South Carolina. Mays himself grew up on a repurposed plantation in Greenwood County, South Carolina, and personally witnessed bigots and the KKK attempting to intimidate his family there.

When I arrived on campus on that cold October day, the nation was still reeling from the police murders of Alton Sterling, Terence Crutcher, and Philando Castile, and students and staff alike were searching for answers. There, with slides, images, and videos, I taught them the story of Leopold von Ranke, the dip, and how human history operates like a roller coaster instead of on a steady upward trajectory of progress. The presentation certainly did not tie up the messy moment we are in with a neat, tidy bow, but it gave the students some essential historical context to understand how we got to this dark place, with hope that we could get out of it if we worked together. During the Q&A following the presentation, a student asked me if I would be willing to tell the audience what they could do to make a difference in the world, now that they understood that we are in a dip. I told them what I just said to you — that they needed to make a decision about the single issue they were going to pour their heart and soul into, and put all of their energy into it.

After I finished the Q&A, a brilliant young student came up to me. Her skin was as dark as night, and she was dressed in a flowing black abaya that went down to her feet, with a hijab covering her hair. After we took a picture together, she looked at me quizzically before posing a question that I quickly sympathized and identified with.

"Mr. King, how can I pick just one issue? I am a Muslim in the age of the Muslim ban. I am from Somalia, a nation that Trump has put on his banned list. I am an immigrant in a nation increasingly harsh to us. I am Black in a nation where racism is very real. I am a woman in a nation of glaring gender inequality and violence. How am I expected to pick just one issue to care about?"

First, my heart broke for her, because I realized in that moment just how privileged I am and how many of the challenges she faces and the fears she must regularly confront I simply will never have. But I also identified with her feeling of caring about so many essential issues as to feel overwhelmed. It's likely that you, too, understand what it feels like to have so many things going on in the world that break your heart or even directly threaten you that some days you just don't know which direction to go.

I first wanted her to understand that her feelings were not just normal, but completely unavoidable. "You are right. You are absolutely right," I told her. "You do not have the luxury of caring about just one cause. You never will. For your entire life, you are always going to feel like you have more battles to fight than you have minutes and hours in the day to fight them. You will always feel, as you fight one battle, that you are missing out on another. I feel this way every day."

I continued on. "Please listen carefully to what I'm saying. You can care about all of these issues, and more. You don't have a choice but to care about so many of them; you care about them for survival. But while you can care about all of these things, you can't fight *effectively* on twenty different issues. Caring about them all, even caring deeply about them all, is fully possible. But one person can only effectively *fight*—and I mean fight in a way that actually makes substantive change—for one cause at a time." She nodded, and seemed relieved above all else. It's overwhelming to have systemic oppression coming at you full force, from multiple directions.

I'm a feeler. I care about the environment. I care about gentrification. I care about childhood literacy and income inequality and universal healthcare and affordable housing and student loan debt and Islamophobia and endless wars and white supremacy and human rights in developing countries. But what I have learned across the years is that, as badly as I wish I could effectively fight for justice on all of those issues, and many more, it's simply impossible. I've tried it. And while each "yes" seemed so noble when I first said it, ultimately a hundred yeses to every cause ended with me being spread so thin that the best I could do for each cause ended up being nothing more than a tweet or a Facebook post—and even those end up being too hurried to actually mean much. But over time I learned that I could find outlets and opportunities for solidarity and support on all of those other issues. Let me share some of those ideas with you here.

The first thing you can do is encourage awareness of other causes. You can care about as many causes as you want, but you can fight only one real battle. I have dozens of causes that I care about, and I make it my mission to amplify them every chance I get. Shout out the experts and leaders in other spaces via your own networks. Maybe that's through social media or by talking to members of your community about these causes. By amplifying, you might end up helping others identify their critical cause. Find ways to support and encourage other people who've already made the decision that I'm asking you to make in all of the various causes that you care about but cannot necessarily commit your energy to full-time.

The second thing you can do is make a financial contribution to other causes. Probably like you, my financial resources are limited, but if you're able, you can set aside a small amount of money each month—the price of a cup of coffee, even—to donate to other causes that are meaningful to you. My wife and I donate to several causes, people, and organizations that we love and trust. We may never be able to volunteer for any of them, but as a leader myself, I know how valuable it is to have monthly donors. For instance, my dear brother Jason, who fought hard against human trafficking in the United States and around the world, passed away in the fall of 2018 after a devastating bout with pancreatic cancer. Until he was diagnosed, I never thought much about pancreatic cancer, but now we give to the leading charity fighting it and have a heightened sensitivity to cancer-related causes. Fighting cancer is not my main cause, but I make sure it's not ignored. You can do the same for other causes that hurt your heart, too.

Lastly, and this is a bit more complex, try to listen carefully and learn how the other causes you care about might

have interesting intersections with the main cause you support. For example, while fighting back against police brutality and mass incarceration in the United States is at the core
of my activism, I've learned much about how the rights of
immigrants intersect with this system. As children and families are snatched away from one another and locked in literal
cages, they are sometimes housed in private prisons owned
by for-profit companies like CoreCivic or the GEO Group,
organizations that I've been fighting against in the justice
system for years. Similarly, when I learned that American
police departments often give training to other police forces
around the world, sometimes even using the same companies for their weapons and surveillance systems, it broad-
ened the geographic scope and interest of my work to study
what was happening in places like Palestine and Brazil.

Do you see the point I'm making? Let me push it a bit
more. I love to read. My wife is an expert when it comes to
literature; education and literacy is her main cause. I don't
have the bandwidth to do substantive, systems-shifting work
in that fight, but I have grown to see at least three ways literacy impacts my work with racial justice and mass incarceration. Here are three key takeaways that I've come across in
my support for Rai's work. First, the average adult entering
an American prison has below a sixth-grade reading level. If
you boost the literacy levels of children, you open up countless doors of opportunity for them and, in the process, di-
vert them away from the school-to-prison pipeline. Second,
prisons are starting to ban books about social justice, like
*The New Jim Crow*—a further extension of state-sponsored
suppression. And, lastly, several studies have shown that of-

ficers with higher levels of educational attainment tend to produce written reports that are better in quality and reliability — *and* they are less likely to engage in police brutality. Understanding how literacy intersects with police brutality and mass incarceration allows me to stay focused on my main cause while adding nuance to the way I approach my activism. This sort of complex, holistic thinking can add extra value to your own fights for justice, while still ensuring that you keep your eye on the prize.

Until you make a serious decision to fight for one single cause, your impact on the world will remain in a holding pattern. I bet you already know what your cause is. You may have even made the decision in your mind a few times but never quite made it official. What I've learned is that most activism doesn't die in the streets; most dreams of changing the world die in our own minds long before we even allow them to materialize. We talk ourselves out of making a difference in the world far more than anybody else talks us out of such a thing. What I want you to understand is that as long as you remain neutral in the face of oppression and danger, your indifference and the collective indifference of millions of others will only allow us to slide deeper into the dip. We won't find our way out of it by accident; climbing that steep mountain is a choice. Right now, as you consider what the cause of your life is going to be and prepare to move forward with it, your mind is going to be flooded with a litany of excuses to derail you. Let's try to debunk those together next.

## 4

# Forget Your Excuses

NOW THAT YOU'VE MADE your decision, we need to have an honest conversation about what may keep you from playing your part in changing the world. Fighting for change is a difficult and often thankless battle, where victories are few and far between — and the prospect of that can be intimidating. Often, when we see an injustice in the world, our minds begin convincing us that we are powerless, that our contribution to the cause won't really matter, that the problem is too deeply entrenched to ever change. Everyone has their own unique fears, challenges, and limitations. Whatever yours are, they can get in the way of leaning into the problems in the world that genuinely trouble you. It's not that these concerns are false; they are each rooted in a very real fear or insecurity that you might have. But our world is in crisis right now. The dip is real. Today's problems — all of them — are going to require you to cast aside your excuses. Let's unpack each of these and then start changing the world together.


## "I'M TOO YOUNG"

This will never be true.

Your youthful zeal and energy, your hopeful and spirited vision, and your willingness to confront powerful people and systems are all needed in the fight for change. Every successful social movement throughout history has had young people at the center of it. The horrible policies and practices we see right now will affect you and your generation more than anyone else. While so many people in power are invested in keeping the systems of this world just the way they are, you know damn well that the status quo is not good enough. And I want you to use that knowledge to fight for the future you deserve.

Have you ever heard of Claudette Colvin? Most people haven't, but she should be a household name. On March 2, 1955, a full nine months before Rosa Parks became known to the world, fifteen-year-old Claudette was arrested for refusing to give up her bus seat to a white woman. As she yelled that it was her constitutional right to have that seat, local police came onto the bus, confronted Claudette, arrested and handcuffed her, and took her to jail. This was *months* before the grown folks did it. Claudette set the stage; her actions were a spark for that city. Young Claudette actually served as one of the plaintiffs in *Browder v. Gayle,* a case that went all the way to the Supreme Court, which eventually determined once and for all that bus segregation in Alabama was unconstitutional.

Eight years later, on May 2, 1963, more than a thousand Black students from all over Birmingham, Alabama, including young elementary school children, walked out of their schools to protest forced segregation and oppression in their city. An astounding 973 children were arrested by police that day—all on the grounds that they did not have a permit for their march. It is widely thought to be the largest mass arrest of children in the entire history of the country. When other children took up the mantle the next day, the bigoted police chief, Bull Connor, ordered that these brave kids be sprayed with fire hoses and met with police dogs. And for *days* these children continued to protest, in the face of all of this danger. As the nation began seeing the horrible images from these events, it put an enormous amount of pressure on Birmingham's white power structure to end the segregation ordinances in their local businesses.

There are so many other examples to find inspiration in. Joan of Arc was just seventeen years old when she bravely stepped up in France to confront the corrupt power structure during the Hundred Years' War. Malala Yousafzai was only eleven when she first became an anonymous blogger for the BBC, detailing what life was like as a young girl in the repressive shadows of the Taliban. Three years after she began doing this, she was shot in an assassination attempt— and even then, she remained committed to her brave stance. Right now, some of the leading voices on climate change, gun control, women's rights, immigration, and so much more are teenagers. Environmental activist Greta Thunberg was just sixteen when she helped lead one of the largest climate strikes in the history of the world. In New York, Luis Hernandez started the brilliant organization Youth Over Guns when he was just sixteen, and he has become one of the most important voices in the nation for stopping gun violence in our communities. The March for Our Lives — which came about in the painful aftermath of seventeen people being shot and killed and seventeen more being injured at Marjory Stoneman Douglas High School, in Parkland, Florida — rallied millions of people together to confront gun violence. It was fueled and organized by high school students.

Young people have been bravely speaking truth to power for thousands of years. Your unique perspective simply can't be duplicated by anybody else. You aren't too young. You are just right.

## "I'M TOO OLD"

This is tough for me to swallow, but when I walk into most rooms full of organizers and activists these days, I am regularly the oldest person in the room. I damn near lost my cool when some teenagers called me an "elder" recently! But it's true. Regardless, we all have a role to play, and we're never too old to start fighting for change. It doesn't matter if you are twice my age — the movement for change needs your wisdom and perspective. It needs your connections and resources. It needs your stories and insight. Put simply, it needs your presence.

In 2018, I was privileged to host a conversation with the

legendary Harry Belafonte. He was ninety-one years old and as sharp as ever. He showed up to the event in a Tray-von Martin hoodie and dropped more wisdom on the audience in an hour than I could in a year. The man was born two years before Dr. King and has found a way to contribute to society into his nineties. For the past twenty years, he has been an indispensable adviser to some of the leading activists in the world.

You aren't too old to fight for change. Not at all. Your ability to bring a multigenerational perspective to the problems of our world is urgently needed.

## "I'M TOO BUSY"

I get it. Some days I'm so busy I feel like my head is going to explode. My schedule is managed down to the minute, from 5 a.m. until 11 p.m. In the eighteen hours I am awake every day, I help lead multiple organizations, record a daily podcast, appear on a nationally syndicated radio show, attend meetings and functions for all five of our kids, write a regular column, fundraise for families and causes, and more. So I understand busy, and I sympathize with the feeling of being overwhelmed.

Here's the key, though: no matter how busy you are, you must schedule actual hardcore time into your daily life to fight for change. If all you gave was 10 percent of your time awake each week to try and enact change—that's about 90 minutes a day—you could probably keep all of your current responsibilities and still find a way to make an impact. But what I am certain of is that it won't happen by accident.

When people tell me they're too busy to fight for this or that, what I really hear is that their schedule isn't optimized as much as it could be. They have time. You and I have time. We just have to use it well. We have to spend less time scrolling on our phones and more time being thoughtful about how we live day to day. Because, as busy as we are, if we ignore our greatest problems, they'll only get worse.

## "I'M TOO WHITE"

If you are reading this and you are white, it's highly likely that your culture, your language, your habits, and your worldview are all much more rooted in the experience of whiteness than you have probably ever considered. It's a good thing that you're thinking about your whiteness before entering spaces where whiteness is not centered. That's a critical point to understand. Because here's the thing: you are needed as an ally, comrade, and co-conspirator in Black spaces, in Latinx spaces, in indigenous spaces, in immigrant spaces. But in doing that, you are going to have to discipline yourself to not expect your whiteness to give you privilege. Over and over again I hear from Black organizers that they regularly experience white allies dropping out of the work when times get tough. I've seen it myself. And it causes an emotional wall of distrust to be put up.

When you enter these spaces, listen more, talk less, get to know the people, and allow them to warm up to you and trust you at their own pace. Be consistent with your presence, and don't bail out if you stumble into a weird moment

or two. Over time, your willingness to learn and your def-
erence to how other cultures operate will win people over,
and you'll find your own organic path within a culture and
community that is not your own.

## "I'M NOT SMART ENOUGH"

It doesn't take a savant or a prodigy to change the world.
It takes determination, time, focus, and a hell of a lot of
hard work, but you don't have to be a damn genius to do
good. If you are brilliant and highly educated, I'm glad for
you. Put all of that knowledge to good use. But I have found
that most colleges and universities don't prepare students to
change the world; they prepare them to maintain it. Don't
get me wrong: I value education and intellect. But having either in excess does not necessarily make someone an agent
of change. You don't have to be the smartest person in the
room to be the most compassionate. You don't have to have
the highest IQ around to be the most generous. Doing good
is far less about aptitude and more about imagination. Are
you able to imagine the world being better and more har-
monious and fair and safe and equitable than it is right now?
Then you can make change.

You and I are smart enough to do this work, and we
are smart enough to make a difference. Whatever knowledge you don't currently possess, you can learn, but do not
dare allow yourself to become frozen in the fear of not being good enough. That's a trick. You are smart enough to
know that the world could be so much better than it is right

now, and to me, that makes you special. The question is not whether you're smart enough to do the work. The question is: How will you use your intellect for good?

## "I DON'T KNOW WHERE TO BEGIN"

I get that. Our biggest problems are both complex and intimidating. And some of them seem so insurmountable, and so deeply entrenched, that it can be hard to know how in the world to begin tackling them. But we cannot allow the size and scale of our world's most difficult problems to intimidate us into inaction.

First, understand that the weight of the entire problem is not on your shoulders. If you care about an issue, I assure you that you're not alone. You need to find an organization or community that shares this burden with you. Try to locate the people who have already made the decision to solve the same problem but are several steps ahead of you. Follow other advocates and organizations behind this cause on social media. See if they have any gatherings or conferences, and join them as a volunteer. Give yourself a month or two to devour every book and article on the topic so that you can wrap your mind around the issue better. Seek out the experts or journalists who've dedicated their lives to solving this problem and read what they have to say about it. Maybe even consider reaching out to them. Just don't check out or move on without pushing yourself first.

And understand this: your entry point into a cause or movement may be wildly different from the next person's. Your story and your past don't have to look anything like mine. You just have to start, plain and simple. Normally, the struggle to know where to begin is more about a lack of knowledge than a lack of direction. Beef up your knowledge and you'll soon be on your way.

## "I DON'T HAVE ENOUGH MONEY"

That's probably true for all of us. Only a few people in the world have enough money to fully fund the changes we need to make. The question you need to ask yourself instead is: Do I have enough money to *start* changing the world today? And the answer to that is yes — seven days a week, twenty-four hours a day. That's because you can be dead broke and unemployed and still make your mind up right now that you are going to make a difference in the world.

What I often find is that good people with good hearts look at the cost of running a world-class organization that will solve the problem and decide that, because they don't have that type of capital, their efforts will be largely unsuccessful. Ultimately, that's a self-fulfilling prophecy. If you don't start doing the work now, with no money and no real budget, with nothing but dreams and elbow grease, you'll never be in a position to obtain the resources you'll eventually need. Take your eyes off the finish line for a few moments and look right in front of your own face. That's where you start. Right where you are. I've never been a full-time activist or organizer. I've always had to work other jobs to provide for my family and give me the space and resources to organize. Every day, I feel like we could do better if we had more money to do the work, but I refuse to allow the lack of resources to keep me from pushing ahead.

## "I'VE TAKEN MY LIFE IN A DIFFERENT DIRECTION"

While it's my dream for each of you to be able to eventually do world-changing work for a living, that's rarely the case for most of us. But the fact that your education, training, or current profession may have taken you in an altogether different direction from the work you feel you need to do to make the world a better place should never keep you from participating in both at the same time. In fact, some of the most brilliant and impactful activists and organizers I know also have a core profession that has little to nothing to do with the causes they've taken up.

In between his roles as Hulk in the *Avengers* movies, the actor Mark Ruffalo fashioned himself into one of the most vocal climate activists in the world. He marches and demonstrates; he visited Standing Rock to show his support for the water protectors there; he fundraises for groups that are doing the work. I see the same thing with NBA superstar LeBron James. As one of the best basketball players of all time, he not only developed one of the largest college scholarship funds ever started by an athlete, but he planned, built, and launched an amazing new school for students from his hometown. And he didn't just write the checks—he was involved in every detail.

But no one needs to be famous in order to find the time and space to work and fight for a cause alongside their regular lives. I see this with everyday people all over the country. Some of the most engaged activists and organizers in the nation have a completely different profession that they lean on to pay the bills. I've seen teachers and nurses become leaders in the fight against police brutality. I've seen college professors become leaders against white supremacy. I've seen fast-food workers become leaders for universal healthcare. I've seen college students become the leading voices battling climate change. And we all saw Alexandria Ocasio-Cortez bravely run for Congress while she was a waitress and bartender. Not only did she win, but she became one of the most influential leaders in the entire government. Wherever you are, whatever direction your life is going in, you are perfectly positioned to make change in the world.

But let me also tell you this: it's okay to completely change course in your life. It's perfectly normal to take a good, hard look at where the world is heading and decide that you want to change majors in college or make a big shift in your career to better reflect your desire to make change. You don't have to do this, of course, but we definitely need people who are fully willing to invest their entire lives in activism efforts. I know the conventional, parental wisdom is to advise people not to do this, but to me, if anything, we need more of this spirit nowadays. Go for it.

## "I DON'T LOOK LIKE AN ACTIVIST"

I'm glad. While I don't quite know what an activist is *supposed* to look like, the good news is that we need people of every look, hue, shape, size, age, culture, nationality, religion, socioeconomic background, sexual orientation, and style to be a part of the movement for change. Our goal is to draw in a critical mass of support from the outside, and that means having a variety of voices and personalities on the inside. So don't get caught up in the fact that you might not have some stereotypical look. There is no look. Be yourself.

Maybe you have it in your mind that activists are a bunch of "cool kids" gathered together, but I assure you, that isn't the case. And I'm not aiming to insult the activist community, because surely a few among us probably are stylish trendsetters, but mainly we are just everyday people, with everyday habits and a wide variety of looks. And we'd be a hell of a lot stronger with you in our ranks. Don't worry about your body size, your hairstyle, your wardrobe, or any of that. Just bring the most authentic version of you to the table!

## "NOBODY BELIEVES IN ME"

Well, *I* believe in you — so that's one person you've already got in your corner. But let me tell you a little secret: it's hard to expect anybody to follow us, or be inspired by us, or believe in us, if we don't fully believe in ourselves first. Self-confidence and self-esteem are contagious. I'm not asking you to "fake it till you make it," but I want you to recognize that you are alive, dammit. You are here for a reason. You are a survivor. You have life lessons and history and skills that matter. And you have every reason to believe in yourself and in your ability to make a difference in the world.

You have a huge heart. You are a dreamer. And those things alone make you unique.

You should never give other people so much power over your life that they can make you think you can't be an effective agent of change. You are better than that. You don't need a fan club to make change; you just need to care more about making a difference than about what anybody else thinks of you. Maybe you're worried about what your friends or family will think when they see you giving your all to a cause that they don't support. Maybe they won't like it, but for all you know, perhaps it'll actually inspire them to see you take your life in this direction. Either way, you can't let that impact you moving forward. There will always be naysayers.

There are a lot of things in the world that we don't get to choose. We don't get to choose when and where we're born. We don't get to choose the cultural context we're born into or the socioeconomic situation of our family. But we can choose our friends. My sincere wish for you is that you have friends who root for you and who believe in your ability to make an impact in this world, friends who'll come along with you and help support and build out your vision for a more just society. Once you find those people, hold them close.

## "I'LL START LATER"

Of all the excuses that people give for not changing the world, none seems as innocuous — while in fact doing more damage — than the good ol' excuse about how we'll start making a difference in the world at some undetermined time in the future. This is a trap. Nine times out of ten, when we tell ourselves we'll start tackling something later, it ends with us doing nothing at all. In some ways, saying *I'll start later* is the lie we tell ourselves because we just don't feel good about acknowledging the truth, which is something more along the lines of *I don't care enough about this problem to interrupt my life and do something about it.*

Listen to me: if you are feeling pulled to make a difference in the world, listen to that gut feeling. That's the best form and expression of yourself. I'm not advising you to chase down every whim, but I am saying that the world and its problems and all of its hurting people damn sure need you and your dedication to a cause. Imagine, just for a moment, that you had listened to that voice inside of your head, admonishing you to take a step toward making change, all the way back when you first heard it. When was that? Probably years ago, right? Imagine how much further along you would be right now if you had acted on that instinct! Well, now I want you to promise that you won't keep delaying and denying your desire to change the world. Because here's the thing: time will keep on ticking, and if you tell yourself again, *Not today but tomorrow,* years will end up passing by.

Our biggest problems in the world may indeed be the result of flawed systems and horribly corrupt individuals, but it's often the ambivalence of the masses that keeps them alive. Whether you intend it to or not, your silence functions as complicity. In many ways, the silence of the masses gives the bad actors and evildoers among us permission to carry on. I know you don't want that, but when you are stuck in a state of delay, that's where you are. So let's change that.

## "I'M AFRAID OF FAILURE"

Let me tell you right now what I wish someone had told me when I was first starting out in my activism efforts: you *are* going to fail. Not because you are insufficient as a person or leader, or because your voice isn't effective. You are going to fail because failure is a part of this process. You won't find a single revolutionary or heroic changemaker anywhere in human history who hasn't failed in countless ways big and small. Did you know that Barack Obama ran for Congress in the year 2000 and lost? It wasn't even *close*. He got creamed, losing 69 percent to 31 percent. Did you know that Oprah Winfrey was fired from her first job as a television news anchor in Baltimore and told that she was "unfit for television"? Could you imagine being the person who said that to Oprah Winfrey? And consider this about author J. K. Rowling. The *Harry Potter* series has sold more than five hundred million copies of its beloved books, but Rowling couldn't even find an agent willing to represent her at first. When she finally did, twelve publishers turned her down before a thirteenth gave her a shot.

Let me tell you about my personal hero, Bernie Sanders. The man never quits. In fact, his legacy is built upon a streak of initial losses. In high school, he ran for student body president and came in last out of three candidates. He waited fourteen years before he ran for office again. In 1972, at the age of thirty-one, he ran for the U.S. Senate in a special election in Vermont but came in last. He ran for governor of Vermont later that same year and again came in last out of three candidates. Two years later, in 1974, he ran again for the U.S. Senate. He came in last out of three candidates, but he quadrupled his support. He ran for governor of Vermont again in 1976, and took up the tail of the race, but he increased his support. That's five straight losses and five straight last-place finishes, but the man still somehow found a glimmer of hope in it all.

Finally, in 1981, Bernie ran for mayor of Burlington, Vermont, and won by ten votes. *Ten!* And guess what happened? He won again in 1983 and 1985, before running for governor in 1986 and getting another loss. Still, he was reelected mayor in 1987, and finally, in 1988, Bernie ran for an open seat in the House of Representatives. Running as an independent, he came in second to the Republican winner, but not by much, and received three times as many votes as he had ever gotten in his life. If you're counting, that was his seventh political campaign loss. He eats losses for breakfast.

When Bernie ran again for Congress in 1990, things turned around and he won, becoming the first independent elected to the House in forty years. The boy who had come in last as student body president in high school then won reelection to Congress in 1992, 1994, 1996, 1998, 2000, 2002, and 2004. In 2006, a full thirty-four years after his last-place finish in his first run for the Senate, Bernie ran for the U.S. Senate and won. He won again in 2012 and yet again in 2018, a year after he was rated the country's most popular politician. And this is all because of his tenacity and his ability to stare failure straight in the face.

So listen: you will lose some battles. Lord knows I've lost my fair share, but they just make the wins that much sweeter. Making change isn't theoretical. You have to get out there and fight for it. You have to be in the game, in the campaign, in the war. Now, I want you to be prepared, but as you'll learn in the next chapter, the best way to learn is by *doing*.

5

# Learn by Doing

NOW, WHEN I WAS IN COLLEGE, I thought I knew a lot about the world, but in August of 2001 my girlfriend and I got the biggest, most surprising news of our lives. She was pregnant. We were damn kids ourselves. Rai had just turned twenty, I was twenty-one, and we were two broke college students in Atlanta at Morehouse and Spelman. We loved each other, of course, and had been together for four years at this point, but this pregnancy was far from planned. We were both first-generation college students and came from families that were counting on us to succeed. We were equal parts nervous, embarrassed, overwhelmed, and excited. We didn't have health insurance. We didn't know the first thing about finding the doctors Rai would need. We didn't have real jobs outside of some small-time work-study positions on campus. We weren't married. And the previous summer had been one of our most challenging ever as a couple.

With nothing but student loan refunds to live off of, we got our first apartment together, bought a few pieces of discount furniture, and started on an entirely unfamiliar path. I clumsily proposed, hoping that Rai would be willing to spend the rest of her life with me. Luckily, she said yes. We both told our mothers, who were far more supportive than we had expected, and prepared to have a private wedding ceremony in the home of Atlanta pastor Howard Creecy, who also served as the chaplain for Atlanta. Reverend Creecy was a Morehouse graduate and had been a mentor of mine for years. Just a few days before we were scheduled to get married, our nation was rocked to its very core.

On a Tuesday morning that September, I had the living room television switched to the *Today* show as I prepared to go to class. When a plane hit the first of the Twin Towers, the hosts began covering the incident with bewilderment, suggesting it was an accident. Seventeen minutes later, when another plane crashed directly into the second tower, it was obvious to the hosts and to all of us that what we were witnessing was not an accident, but an unspeakable act of terror. When a third plane crashed into the Pentagon and there were reports of a fourth plane heading toward the nation's capital, it became unmistakably clear that the whole country was under attack.

By this time in her pregnancy, Rai was already experiencing the morning sickness from hell, except it wasn't just limited to the morning — she was nauseous around the clock. As a result, she was in bed resting as I witnessed the terror unfolding on live television. While I normally prided myself on letting her rest no matter the circumstances, in this instance I felt that I needed to go wake her to tell her that something truly horrible was happening in our country. As we watched that awful, wrenching footage huddled together, I began wondering about what kind of crazy world we were about to bring a child into.

Like thousands of couples all across the country, Rai and I canceled our small wedding that was planned for the weekend after 9/11. Instead, eleven days later, with Rai so sick that she could hardly get out of bed, we got married in a simple ceremony at Reverend Creecy's house. When it was over, we felt like two brand-new people, I swear to you. We had committed ourselves to each other for the rest of our lives. It gave us both a strange sense of peace and calmness to know that we'd never be alone. We were giddy and giggly about it for days on end.

Then reality fully set in. We needed to figure out how to provide for ourselves and how to care for Rai and the baby-to-be. Student loan refunds weren't going to cut it. As a result, I got a full-time job doing airport security. They were hiring anybody who passed a background check in those days; I literally started work the day after I was hired. On the days I didn't have class, I worked sixteen-hour shifts at Peachtree-Dekalb Airport. Rai would pack me a cooler full of meals, drinks, and snacks, and on my breaks I'd cram in my homework and call to check on her every chance I got. We found doctors for Rai but couldn't afford the visits. Our income was so low that we qualified for both Medicaid and food stamps. It took days of interviews to finally get approved for both, but these services were lifesavers. We could not have made it without them. As young, naive, and broke as we were, we were also as satisfied and happy as two people could ever be. It was one of the sweetest times of our entire marriage.

We had held babies before, and even changed a diaper or two, but we didn't know the first thing about pregnancy, childbirth, or what it took to actually raise a tiny little human. So we did what college students do: we bought books. We read everything we could get our hands on, from books that broke down the pregnancy week by week to parenting manuals that explained "everything" you would ever need to know once your baby arrived. We took childbirth classes together. We kept a diary charting all of the milestones of the pregnancy. And we asked countless questions at every doctor's appointment.

By the time Rai was full-term, her belly had grown to be so big that people regularly asked us if we were having twins. Just as the books said to do, we had our emergency bag packed and ready next to the door. On the evening of March 17, when Rai began having strong contractions, we went to the hospital. She was in labor for hours and hours and hours. I had practiced breathing and counting with her for weeks, but we never even used it. After nearly sixteen hours, the doctors decided that Rai would need a C-section. None of this was going according to plan; our books hardly even mentioned C-sections, or the possibility of being in labor for sixteen hours. We trusted our doctors but soon found ourselves in a place that our research had not quite prepared us for. I was in the operating room with Rai as they performed the C-section. I will spare you the gory details, but it is an extreme surgery that is talked about flippantly as if it is something simple to endure and recover from. Neither of those is true. Rai was in pain for weeks. Again, our books had failed us.

When we got home from the hospital with little baby Kendi, Rai could hardly walk up the stairs to our second-floor apartment. Our house was overrun with family and friends when what Rai and the baby truly needed was peace and quiet. When everybody finally left and it was just us, we were relieved. One of the first things we said to each other was "Books didn't explain any of this shit."

Not a single one of our friends from Morehouse and Spelman was a parent. Nobody in our entire local ecosystem had kids. We had jumped the timeline and were really on our own to figure things out. When it came time to give Kendi her first bath, we got it all set up for her. She had her own little bathtub, with a soft little water cushion to make her comfortable. We filled the tiny tub with gentle soap and water, got her undressed, and sat her on the cushion. Suddenly she started screaming bloody murder. She was a sweet, quiet baby, so the screams alarmed us. Rai got the washcloth and gently rubbed water across her, but she just screamed even more. We couldn't make sense of it. It was almost as if she were allergic to water.

She wasn't. The water was just cold. It wasn't ice-cold, but colder than what a baby would ever want, and my dumb ass had not yet perfected the science of pouring perfect bathwater. To be fair, it's no easy feat. Too hot and you scald them, too cold and they scold you. It wasn't until we ran her a bath the next day and made the water warmer that we figured out our foolish error. Like every baby, she loved warm baths, but we had just gotten the temperature wrong that first time.

Over the years, as we've parented our five kids, we've found that they've sent us on more surprising twists and turns in the process than we ever could've imagined. Don't get me wrong: the journey has been beautiful. But every step of the way, we've learned that the best manual in the world wouldn't be enough to help prepare us. The books and eventually the videos and podcasts on parenting that we've devoured over the years have given us some base knowledge, but what we've come to understand is that the hardest things in parenting are best learned by actually doing them.

The same principle applies to most activities in life, from shooting a basketball to painting a picture to filming a movie to knitting a scarf. You can read about those things all you want, but nothing is going to compare with the actual process of *doing* the thing you're trying to learn about over and over and over again until you start to pick up the skills, improve them, and make the craft your own. Hear me clearly: I want you to read every book you can on changing the world and making it a better place. But if you just read books about making change, including this one, and don't actually go out and take the risks that need to be taken, you will be well-read, but the world will be no better for it. Eventually you are going to have to close this book, put down the phone, and get to work.

When you first get started, you are bound to be as overwhelmed and unsure as I was when I put a calm baby in cold water and got the reaction that I did. It happens. When I did that, I still had to give the baby a bath the next day and the next one and the next one. By the time the fifth and final baby came around, every adult and child in our house knew how to run a bath and bathe an infant. You get good at a skill, then you spread the word and responsibilities to those around you. That's how making change works.

Now that you've chosen your cause and pushed past your excuses, I want to help you understand exactly what's going to come next, because it's a fragile, vulnerable place for you and for the cause you aim to support. As I write this book, I still find it outrageously difficult to go from caring about a problem in the world to becoming a meaningful volunteer and advocate on behalf of a hardcore solution. The on-ramp to go from caring to serving is a clumsy, confusing one. I just need to emphasize that before we even begin.

What I am asking from you right now is to be very patient in the early days of trying to figure out how to make change. It's going to be frustrating sometimes, but I want to share some useful tips that might help you on your journey. First, do some research on the leading national and local organizations for your cause. Find and follow on social media all of the organizations and leaders doing the work that you hope to do yourself; follow whom they follow. Study who they seem to respect and amplify. Eventually you'll start to notice the difference between who's doing real work and who's just out here talking about it. Go to the websites of the organizations and campaigns that you respect and study them. See if they have platforms and plans or a detailed policy agenda. When organizations and campaigns have these, understand that what you are looking at may look simple, but is likely the culmination of months and months, even years, of hard work. Take the time to study those documents. Download them if that's possible and make a point of reading, understanding, and digesting information so that you could repeat back at least some of the main points intelligently if you were put on the spot.

While you are on a website, there are some things I'd like you to do. First, see if the organization has local chapters or offices. It's going to be way easier to volunteer on the local level than it ever would on the national level, and those types of localized, grassroots efforts are essential. Check out whether they have a public calendar of events on their website. These websites are frequently outdated, so if you don't see such a thing, follow their social media accounts and see whether they have any public events listed in your neck of the woods. When you see a meeting or event on the schedule, make a commitment to go. Shake off your nerves and doubt, and take your desire to fight for change public. Trust me, when leaders have events, we never know if they are going to be packed or sparse, so we really treasure each and every person who shows up. Feel free to introduce yourself to people there. Don't be pushy to the point of weirdness, but exchange information, and let them know that you are hoping to volunteer alongside them and could start immediately.

Make sure to check out what their volunteer process looks like, too. The organization's website will likely lead you to a more formal process for getting you on board. Sign up, but understand that most organizations don't have full-time volunteer coordinators. In a dream world, you'd sign up to volunteer and immediately get a phone call or personal email telling you what's next, but it rarely works that way. If it does, treat the person who replies to you like gold. They are a gatekeeper and are doing vital work for the cause. If you get an automated reply to your email, try replying to it with a short message to simply let them know who you are and how you'd *really* like to volunteer for the cause. If a real person replies to your message, again, treat them like gold. They've been given an important task and are going to appreciate your warmth and kindness. You can even offer to hop on the phone to introduce yourself. Organizations and campaigns are often overwhelmed with both work and noise, and sometimes you have to find a way to cut through it all to make it clear that you are a real person who is ready to help make a difference alongside them.

Doing all of this *could* get your foot in the door. It should be enough, of course, but again, organizations often struggle with this onboarding process. Don't take it as a personal insult if you work hard to get a reply from an organization or campaign and just don't get it. Most of us are simply overwhelmed from day to day and are doing our very best to reply when we can. The irony of it all is that we need you, but we often lack the bandwidth to help you take the next step. Have patience with these organizations, particularly young ones in development.

But let's assume you *do* get a reply and are offered a chance to become a volunteer. That's great! Let me hold your hand through this next part: Please, please don't make this hard for the volunteer coordinator. If they tell you that they have two dates and times available to train volunteers, please try your best to make your schedule work with one of those slots instead of asking if they can make another time available for you. It may require you to use a vacation day or to shift your schedule around, but doing so will increase the likelihood that you are actually going to get involved in a meaningful way, and that's the goal here. When an organization or campaign has taken the time to create a volunteer process and interested people don't follow it, it can overwhelm the system and lead to less effective organizing. Even high-functioning organizations and campaigns often don't have contingency plans that account for people who opt out of the systems that are put in place, so please respect the process.

Whether or not you get to attend a volunteer training, an interest meeting, a private gathering, a public protest, or a face-to-face meeting with an executive in an organization, please, pretty please, don't ask if they are hiring—especially not in your first meeting or two. Even if you mean well, you will run the real risk of coloring the way people in the organization will think about you moving forward. It will give everyone the impression that you aren't there for the cause, but for the employment opportunity. They will question the integrity of your motives and assume that the extent of your commitment begins and ends with being paid for the work. Even if you ultimately hope to one day work for this organization, make a strong impression first. Complete the volunteer training. Become a volunteer. And then see where that takes you.

Similarly, when you set out to serve an organization or campaign, don't make rising up through the ranks your main objective. The United States is heavily driven by corporate capitalism. The thing is, the principles of corporate capitalism, where the primary objective is profit, often at all costs, are not the same principles required to make change. In corporate capitalist systems, positions and titles often mean everything, but successful movements for change function with completely different metrics and operational paradigms. Their goal is not profit or status or title or credit; their sole goal is change. And when your true goal is deep, systemic change, you will slowly begin to unlearn the corporate cultures that have been imposed upon us all. If an organization starts to take on a traditional corporate framework, it will ultimately begin to exist simply to support itself more than to support the fight for change. Off the top of my head, I could name a dozen organizations that now exist and function mainly to support their continued existence, instead of existing to bring about the social change they claim to have been created to fight for. If that's the case with the organization you're volunteering for—and you can check sites like GuideStar for donation breakdowns—perhaps you should look for a different way to support your cause.

As a new volunteer, you don't need to be a silent observer, but you should do way more listening and learning in those early days than anything else. Ask questions. Take notes. It's not just a sign of respect; it will allow you to build a strong, accurate base to work from. As urgent as so many of our problems truly are, the deeper the knowledge and wisdom base you build in the early days of your service, the sharper your impact will be. Knowledge is like a slingshot to social change. Every lesson and detail learned is like pulling back the band, increasing your strength, so when it's time for you to get to work, your actions will go so much further, and your impact will be so much greater, as a result.

When you do take those steps, your initial volunteer opportunities might not look like your most audacious dreams of changemaking. Change rarely feels that grandiose. Based on my personal experience throughout the years, here are some of the things you might be asked to do:

- Data entry
- Taking meeting attendance
- Printing copies of the agenda
- Bringing dry-erase markers or Sharpies
- Ushering an event and helping with crowd control
- Being in charge of snacks and refreshments
- Helping pass out flyers or getting petitions signed
- Being a stage manager or helping guard a door
- Managing a social media account
- Keeping a website updated
- Taking photos of events
- Surveying the crowd to make sure that everyone with a disability gets proper seating
- Cleaning up before or after an event
- Serving as a translator for another language
- Phone banking to call complete strangers to persuade them to come to your side of an issue
- Sending text messages to strangers to try your best to persuade them to join the cause
- Canvassing neighborhoods — knocking on the doors of more strangers to see if they, too, will join the cause

These are only some of the important but less-than-glamorous tasks that can help an organization run smoothly.

Do these things with pride. Change requires all of these tasks and so much more.

The truth is that you might not know quite what your role is going to be in making change, but I wouldn't let that initial lack of clarity cause you to delay taking the first step. What I have found is that with every step I take, the clarity comes with the work itself. The closer you are in proximity to the movement and the fight and the struggle, the better you will understand what roles you are likely to play. And these roles will likely change for you. You'll change, too, but please don't despise the days of small beginnings. We can never be too humble in our fight together.

And remember: keep an open mind and an open heart. When you take the initial steps toward change, you never know what new doors might open and what substantive relationships and bonds may form as a result of your work. Had I not reached out one day after the 2016 election to tell the organizer Becky Bond how much I loved her book *Rules for Revolutionaries*, I don't know that if I would've ended up serving as a co-founder of the Real Justice PAC. That work has been some of the most meaningful, impactful work of my life and has sparked some of the most vital friendships I've ever had. Similarly, had I not had years of rich conversations with award-winning journalists Glenn Greenwald and Jeremy Scahill after first reaching out through Twitter DMs, I might never have gotten the opportunity to join them on the writing staff of *The Intercept*. I didn't befriend them with such an opportunity in mind, but it came about nonetheless. I learned so damn much about investigative journalism during my years there.

At this point, I am a confident early adopter. I will gladly take the first step to support a candidate or a cause before it's popular or trendy. That's a learned behavior that I've grown into, but by getting out into the world and actually doing the work, I've discovered more about myself — and about how change is truly made — than I ever could have learned by just reading about it and wondering what was possible. Again, I'm not telling you to read less; I'm telling you to *do* more. And I promise that once you get outside of your shell and push past your fears, then all of the books on changemaking and changemakers are going to feel brand-new to you. You won't read and experience them as a voyeuristic outsider; you will now see the freedom fighters from throughout history as your fellow travelers.

After you get your feet under you in the cause, doing the necessary grunt work in the beginning, you will eventually be able to transition into the next phase of your life as a change agent. This is where you can bring all of your unique skills, gifts, passions, and training to bear. When we first enter into service for a cause, we are rarely in our sweet spot. But my dream for you is that you will find your way there. Let's talk about how that's possible.

## 6

# What Is Your Gift? Use It.

LONG BEFORE TWITTER, before hashtags and trending topics, when the word "viral" was used primarily to describe a disease, I was a pastor. For the first fifteen years of my life, nobody in my universe ever would've predicted such a thing. I hated church. My mother did, too. She worked like a dog at the lightbulb factory and cherished having a day where she did nothing but rest. Sunday was our day to sleep in, and we *loved* it. When people would occasionally ask me what church I attended, I'd flash them a sly grin and say, "Bedside Baptist."

For most of my childhood, Black families in my hometown would invite me to attend church services or Vacation Bible School during the summer break. VBS was a weeklong program where kids would be given snacks, do a religious arts-and-crafts activity, then be taught a short Bible lesson. Unbeknownst to me, families were encouraged to invite their unsaved, nonreligious friends to VBS with the hope that the program would convert them. Consequently, I was there every year. I'd drink the Capri Sun and eat the animal cookies, but I would always leave the religion behind.

Though I was indifferent to organized religion, I had a general belief in God. But as I started experiencing the harassment and cruelty day in and day out as a student at Woodford County High School, that flimsy belief was being tested. *What God,* I wondered to myself, *would see me, hear my cries, see the abuse, and then choose to do nothing?* As the frequency and severity of the abuse got worse, and it seemed like no compassionate adult even cared enough to intervene, I found myself uttering simple prayers, desperate for any sort of sign from the universe. "Please make it stop. God, if you can hear me, please help," I'd say. Nothing changed. Nothing at all. "God, please protect me. I don't want to die," I'd pray. But the abuse continued. Hell, my feeble prayers seemed to make it worse!

After I was assaulted, I missed nearly two years of school while I recovered from the injuries and subsequent surgeries. It was a painful, terrible time, and I didn't want a single soul to see me in that condition. I encouraged my mother to tell my friends who would come visit that I was asleep or in too much pain to talk. After a while, most of them got the message and stopped dropping by. But my best friend, Willis, was the exception. We had known each other since kindergarten but had gotten particularly close over the previous year, and I felt comfortable letting my guard down around him. He would check on me whenever he could, and he always had a way of making me laugh despite the circumstances.

One day, his father, Reverend Willis Polk, decided to come visit me as I recovered in bed. Reverend Polk was one of the most respected people in town, an affable man who pastored at one of the largest Black churches in Lexington. But in that room, he was more like a father to me than anything else. He seemed strangely confident that I would get through this hard time, but he also wasn't shy about talking openly to me about my pain. During one of these conversations, as he got ready to leave, he grabbed my hand and offered to pray for me. Nobody in my entire life had ever prayed for me, at least not out loud so I could hear them. I agreed, my hope being that if God would not hear my prayers, then God would at least hear them from Reverend Polk. I was surprised by what I heard. Reverend Polk talked to God in plainspoken English; he didn't code-switch from the voice he used to speak to me to the voice he used to speak to God. Over the years I had wondered if I was praying wrong, but this man's relatable prayers made perfect sense to me. As he asked God for the healing of my body, mind, and soul, I found myself yearning for it all to be possible. In one vulnerable moment, my heart softened to faith in a higher being.

Late the following spring, before I was even well enough to return to school, I started going to church with the Polk family on Sunday mornings. By that summer, I asked to go every chance I could. And not just to Sunday service, either. I attended planning meetings, choir rehearsals, and Bible studies. It was in those meetings and rehearsals that I met the cutest girl I had ever seen—a spunky, fashionable youth leader named Rai-Tonicia Adams, the woman who would eventually become my best friend and wife. I got baptized a few months after I started attending Antioch Missionary Baptist Church, and a year after that, as a seventeen-year-old boy, I became a licensed preacher, the youngest ever from our church. For the first time in my life, I felt like I had a mission and a real sense of direction. The church mothers, as we called them, like Ms. Iona and Ms. Alberta, helped love me back to life. My own dear mother was relentless in her love for me, but suddenly I had an entire church full of people who saw my potential and had hope for my future. Grown men like Jerry, Beau, and Geno would look me right in the eye and tell me that they *knew* I was going to be somebody. After years of feeling like I might not even live long enough to make it out of Versailles, their affirmations were like medicine to my soul.

When I finally left Versailles for Morehouse in August of 1997, I was one of the most serious, determined, focused teenagers you could ever meet. I was ready for the next chapter, supported by my newfound faith and community. In fact, Reverend Polk himself was the one who took me to visit Morehouse, convinced that both Willis and I would love it. He was right. Just a few weeks into freshman year, after moving into the tiny dorm room with Willis, I learned that my public speaking experience as a young preacher would open doors for me on campus. At Morehouse, public speaking was seen as a kind of social currency, a step toward bigger leadership roles. I started speaking at events around campus almost immediately. Within two weeks, I was elected dorm president, and within a few months I was speaking at political rallies and religious events at colleges all across the city. Speaking energized me. Coming from a high school that would not dare put a microphone in front of my face, I was so damn honored that people all over campus were coming out to hear me speak.

When I decided to participate in the college-wide Otis Moss Jr. Oratorical Contest in March of 1999, I was far from the only teenage preacher. About thirty-five of us entered the first round, which was held in the same small chapel, Sale Hall, that a teenage Martin Luther King Jr. had attended daily as a student at Morehouse fifty years earlier. We were each given the same prompt—something generic about making progress in the impending millennium—and were asked to interpret it in our own unique way, in four minutes or less. I had nearly mastered speaking in front of a crowd for applause and impact, but the idea of speaking to a silent group of judges freaked me out. I had prepared over the previous few days, but I still very much needed my script. When it came my turn, I nailed the delivery and substance but didn't even get to finish my conclusion before the time-keeper signaled that I had hit my limit.

Thankfully, I still made the finals, leading to what was, at that time, the single biggest moment of my academic career. Ten of us were set to compete in front of the entire student body of Morehouse College in the famed King Chapel, a regal, cavernous space that seated precisely 2,501 people —not 2,500, but 2,501, because Dr. King always believed you could fit in one more person. The contest was scheduled to happen during our mandatory campus-wide weekly Thursday morning service, the Crown Forum. While the size and scale of the chapel was intimidating, it was the audience that made speaking there either exhilarating or excruciating, depending on just how skilled you were at connecting with the crowd. All 2,501 seats would be filled for that chapel service, and if the speaker bombed, it was like *Showtime at the Apollo,* where the crowd boos certain Amateur Night acts until a dancing jester with a cane comes and drags them off the stage. Brothers would regularly snicker or even laugh out loud if a speaker mispronounced a name or a word. If a speaker stuttered or bombed in some way, students would be in stitches.

It was in that auditorium that one of us was going to be crowned the best orator on campus. Before the program began, the participants gathered backstage in the chapel office. I loved that space so much. It was covered from floor to ceiling with images and memorabilia from throughout the history of Morehouse. The dean of the chapel, Dr. Lawrence Carter, was as regal and dignified as the chapel itself. I had been a chapel assistant under his tutelage off and on for the previous two years, and hoped to make him proud. As I sat backstage waiting, with sweaty palms and a dry mouth, I suddenly got the feeling that the other students were better prepared than me. But before I could dwell on that too much, the host of the program, Dr. Anne Watts—who had the most exacting diction of anyone I had ever heard— came to tell us to get in line.

King Chapel was packed, and the energy in the room was electric. You could feel it in the air. I was fourth in line, set to deliver a speech that was a blend of hip-hop and revolutionary politics. The students who went before me each performed well, but they didn't connect with the audience. When it was my turn, I took a sip of water, tried to calm my nerves, and then launched into it. Almost as soon as I started speaking, I fell into the flow. I tried to channel the energy of Malcolm X — not just his seriousness, but also his comfort and confidence. I didn't write my speech to win the award, though; I wrote it to win the crowd. I injected references to rap and included stories with illustrations from student life that I knew would resonate, and everyone loved it. When I finished, students jumped to their feet for a raucous standing ovation. As I went back to my seat and played it cool, the broken boy in me who had overcome so much to even make it to Morehouse wanted to cry tears of joy. Instead, I held it together. We wouldn't learn the winner of the contest until the following Thursday, but I felt great about my performance and the audience's reaction.

The next week, before a huge faction of the student body, Dr. Watts announced that I had indeed won the first annual Otis Moss Jr. Oratorical Contest. Winning changed my life: I received a $500 prize, which I used that day to buy my first-ever laptop. But more important, it got me hooked on public speaking and showed me that I could use the skill to inspire and inform audiences and point them to social change.

Winning instantly catapulted me into being seen as one of the preeminent leaders on campus. In many ways, Morehouse students saw speaking well and leading well as interchangeable. Our heroes, like Dr. King and Malcolm X, were known as phenomenal speakers, and many of us saw persuasive oratorical skills as the first sign of leadership. We were too young and dumb to understand how much more went into being an effective leader. I'd later learn that you could crush it on the microphone and not really know the first thing about leading people.

After the victory, I was so full of adrenaline and confidence that I decided to do something virtually unheard of: I ran for student government president as a nineteen-year-old sophomore. It was a long-standing unspoken rule at the time that you ran only as a junior, so that you would be a senior when you were president. The blowback from upperclassmen was fierce. Campus politics were cutthroat, and some of the students I was running against suggested that I was violating the rules by even being in the race. I knew that in order for me to win, it wouldn't be enough to just nail all of the debates; I was going to have to outwork my opponents in every other way. I literally knocked on every single door on every floor of every dorm, some more than once. My promise to the students was to push the school to teach from a more Afrocentric lens and to commit myself, as a representative of my fellow students, to fighting the racial inequality we saw in the world and around our campus. I would be an activist president. That messaging worked. In 1999, I became the first teenager and the first sophomore to win the position since the young scholar Dr. Samuel DuBois Cook won back in 1946–47, and the first student in at least a decade to win the crowded contest without a runoff.

Public speaking became a huge part of my life and leadership. While an undergrad, I was asked to speak at elementary, middle, and high schools all across Atlanta. Former Atlanta mayor Maynard Jackson, who was also a Morehouse

Man, took me under his wing and began introducing me to local and national political figures. Eventually I was asked to speak at political rallies for Al Gore in his campaign for president, and I started doing media interviews on CNN and with other press outlets. It was based on my reputation as a public speaker that I was hired in 2004 to travel and speak full-time at jails and prisons throughout Georgia, which I did nonstop, several times a day, five days a week, for years. There, I taught violence prevention, stress management, goal setting, and breathing techniques, using storytelling as a means to drive thoughtful conversation.

Speaking is a natural skill that I've honed and improved with thousands and thousands of hours of practice, preparation, and delivery. At this point, I've delivered keynotes at Google, Facebook, and Spotify, at Harvard, Princeton, and Yale, but I've also spoken in dozens of the hardest jails and prisons in our nation. I've spoken before crowds of tens of thousands of people in arenas and at political rallies, but I have put in the exact same effort to speak on street corners in Brooklyn with no microphone. I promise I'm not just saying all this to brag. I want to share this part of my journey with you because I need you, too, to drill down and determine what your greatest skills and gifts are. Because after you answer the question of what the single most important social issue is going to be in your world, and you get in the room and learn the nuances of your cause's mission, structure, and purpose, the next questions you need to ask yourself are: *What unique skills and training and expertise do I have, and how can I leverage that for social good? What is the one thing*

*I love doing so much that I would do it for free? What do I do in the world that brings me joy? What gives me energy? What is the thing I most look forward to doing, so that when I do it, it does not feel like a chore but more like liberation?*

I suggest you take to heart some words from the beloved theologian Howard Thurman. Dr. King was said to have carried Thurman's book *Jesus and the Disinherited* in his pocket throughout the Montgomery Bus Boycott. Thurman said, "Don't ask yourself what the world needs. Ask yourself what makes you come alive, and go do that, because what the world needs is people who have come alive." What makes each and every one of us come alive is as unique to us as our fingerprints. What makes me come fully alive is deeply rooted in my own life, and what makes you come fully alive is deeply rooted in yours. Once you know the cause you want to support, you need to assess what gift, talent, or skill you can bring to the table to help amplify your efforts. Public speaking is that for me. What is it for you? Maybe it's obvious, or maybe you're just now getting a handle on your skills and gifts. I promise you they are there, within you, waiting to be tapped and developed to make change.

My greatest dream for you is that you will be able to one day use your greatest skills and gifts to impact the cause that breaks your heart. I am asking you to do this introspective work in these early days of your changemaking so that you can one day have the peace of mind of knowing that every ounce of your energy was used effectively to get us out of the dip we find ourselves in. Of course, you don't have it all figured out right now. Thank goodness that's not a requirement to do good. This world needs you, and there is room for *everyone* in the fight to make change, at every stage. This battle is going to take all of us. Winning a war always does.

It takes writers and editors.
It takes policy analysts and lobbyists.
It takes finance experts and fundraisers.
It takes graphic designers and webmasters.
It takes filmmakers and producers.
It takes data scientists and managers.
It takes skilled leaders and organizers.
It takes drivers and movers.
It takes cleaners and packers.

It takes speakers and singers.
It takes protesters and demonstrators.
It takes artists and dreamers.
It takes farmers and chefs.
It takes urban planners and engineers.
It takes lawyers and judges.
It takes nurses and doctors.
It takes preachers and healers.
It takes counselors and therapists.
It takes teachers and mentors.

Know that whatever your skill is—accounting, filmmaking, event planning, graphic design, legal work—you can put it to good use. It may be your job at this moment or work you do on the side or a hobby that makes you happy. Think deeply on this. It's incredibly important to be realistic and honest with yourself in this process. This will save you great amounts of frustration and angst and prevent you from getting in over your head by committing to play a role that looks good on paper but feels disingenuous in your heart. If you are shy and get anxious speaking in front of crowds, then you don't have to hold the megaphone at a rally. Maybe you're not a numbers person; or maybe you're creative as hell but you're not very organized. All of that is okay. One role is not better than another, and so whatever your gift is, bring it to the table. There's room for you here.

*Part Three*

# What Every
# Movement Needs

WE WANT CHANGE — in fact, we *need* change — but desiring it and actually making it happen are two totally different propositions. Shifting systems, creating sweeping new laws and policies, reversing societal trends and culture, amending the Constitution, convicting violent cops, and ousting corrupt politicians and replacing them with bold new ones — it's all damn near impossible. The odds stacked against us are so severe, our opposition so deeply embedded and well funded, that even in the face of gut-wrenching, life-or-death problems, change only slowly drips out, drop by drop, like water from a leaky faucet. But it can and must happen.

After fighting against police brutality and mass incarceration like my life depended on it in 2014 and 2015, and surrounding myself with families and entire communities that did the very same thing, only to see very little tangible, measurable change come as a result, I went searching down a path for how change is actually made. I studied successful social movements and societal breakthroughs from throughout history. I traveled to forty-five states across the country and broke bread and huddled up with brilliant leaders from a variety of movements for civil and human rights around the world. And most of all, I took a deep, introspective look at my own failures and drastically shifted my methods and approach to changemaking.

At the center of it all, there is a persistent belief that must be confronted: we have greatly overestimated the practical value of being *good* and being *right* when it comes to making change. Being on the right side of history is not good enough. Having the moral high ground is not good enough. Having integrity is not good enough. Don't misunderstand me: we should have all of those things. But the fact of the matter is that we can be right and good and moral, and still *lose* —and I mean in perpetuity—because goodness alone will not create systemic change. If simply being morally right were enough to win elections or change laws or stop human rights violations, the world would be a very different place. But we have profoundly exaggerated the political benefits of being right, at the expense of the hardcore organizing work that is required to actually win.

Let's be on the right side of the most important issues of our time, absolutely, but please recognize that's just the starting point. Now we must strategically organize ourselves out of the deep dip we find ourselves in. Here's how we can do it . . .

# 7

# Energized People

THIS MAY NOT COME as a surprise to you, considering what you've read so far in this book, but I need to circle back to a point that I cannot emphasize enough: politicians and corporations designed and built the status quo that we are living in. It's not a grand accident. It took hundreds of years, thousands even, to craft the current social order. It is complex, and it is directly linked to keeping certain people in power and preventing others from ever threatening it. Consequently, it is enforced, defended, and protected at great expense. And when you even attempt to tinker with the status quo, the pushback you are going to receive will be fierce.

The status quo is not a passive, invisible force. It is Godzilla. It is King Kong. It is a nearly invincible monster that protects the power and privilege not just of a few elite billionaires, but of millions of people who also benefit from it. Gun violence, mass incarceration, voter suppression, the

climate crisis, income inequality, white supremacist terror-
ism, the rising costs of healthcare—all of those issues exist
as deeply entrenched aspects of our everyday lives because
real people fight behind the scenes to make sure these structures remain intact. They profit off of our pain; our despair
is their dividend. And they will do anything in their power
to keep it that way. These people won't fight fair. As we've
seen, they rarely play by the rules. And if we don't shift how
we fight, they will win, again and again.

Even if you've picked your cause and know what issue
is closest to your heart, the gravitational pull of the status
quo is real for all of us. Call it "the rat race" or "the nine-to-
five" or whatever you want, but all of us, on one level or another, have opted in and accept our day-to-day realities. Day
in and day out, we all have jobs, responsibilities, bills, needs,
appointments, and an excess of distractions that have absolutely nothing to do with the causes that we care about. But
in order to make change, we absolutely must set aside our
own routines, harness those moments of despair, anger, and
hopelessness, and channel it all into tangible action.

If we are going to impact the world in measurable ways
and interrupt the status quo, the first step is making sure
that there are *highly energized* people in every social movement. This is easier said than done. Our movement has to
have so much energy that it interrupts it for everyday people
around the globe. Our work has to be so highly energized
that it basically hacks into the central database of people's
lives and forces itself into their daily schedules.

I'm sorry to have to go all science fiction on you for a moment, but let me try and illustrate what highly energized

people do for a cause. Imagine for a moment that the status quo acts as an invisible force field that blocks all possible pathways to change. Then imagine that every single time somebody tries to take the nation down a different, more equitable path . . . *boom!* All of the forces that are beholden to the status quo block the action. It's when scores of highly energized people come together, determined to make change, that they basically blast a hole through that force field and create a temporary portal for changemakers to walk through. That portal doesn't stay open indefinitely, but it's in these moments that the potential to meaningfully shift systems becomes supercharged.

Energy in social movements is often reactionary. Of course, we must always aim to be proactive in our pursuit of change, but sometimes—particularly when we're faced with a horrible act of violence or oppression, like a school shooting or a high-profile act of police brutality—we enter into a rare space where the desperate calls for change spread like wildfire. Yes, it's a place of pain and anguish—trauma, even—but it's often in that very time and space where the possibility of change is the greatest. All change is contextual. It doesn't happen in spite of the times, but in direct response to the felt reality of everyday people. And whatever change we are going to see, it's bound to emanate from this active base.

That's exactly what happened in the summer and fall of 2014, after the police murders of Eric Garner, John Crawford III, Michael Brown, Ezell Ford, and Tamir Rice. Their brutal deaths brought feelings of grief, anger, and despair to their families and friends and communities, but they also ushered in a moment where the status quo became examined and scrutinized. Energized people made that happen. The families of the victims made that happen. Local activists and organizers throughout the country, in small towns and huge metropolises, made that happen. It started with that base, passionately advocating and agitating for justice, and because of their tireless efforts, word eventually spread across the country. Soon enough, #BlackLivesMatter moved from being a hashtag and trending topic to an on-the-ground movement of highly energized, informed people around the world. In the wake of those horrific murders, marches and demonstrations took over entire cities and college campuses across the United States. Highways were shut down. Offices were blocked. Celebrities, athletes, and entertainers joined in, raising Black Power fists before games and events, wearing T-shirts that said I CAN'T BREATHE or BLACK LIVES MATTER, and mentioning the cause in interviews and award-show acceptance speeches. And as a result of this energy, that hole in the force field of the status quo grew slightly bigger day by day, and momentum for real, substantive change continued to build.

For an entire year, from July of 2014, with the murder of Eric Garner, through July of 2015, with the wrongful arrest and in-custody death of Sandra Bland in rural Texas, police brutality not only dominated the news cycle, but it was arguably the single most discussed policy issue in the nation. Police brutality had been present in American culture for generations, but it wasn't until this highly energized movement emerged that the crisis of police violence was finally treated like a public policy emergency. For a small window of time, it felt like the force field that protected the systems and structures of police brutality had their defenses down. And as a result of the collective outcry, several meaningful steps to begin addressing the crisis were taken. President Obama formed a White House task force on police reform. The Justice Department announced that it was investigating many of the most prominent cases of police brutality for civil rights violations. Several big-city mayors and congresspeople began speaking out about the injustices and even joined many of the protests around the country. Progress seemed inevitable.

And yet, even with all of that energy, with all of that media coverage, with all of that forward momentum, not a single one of the families that the Black Lives Matter movement advocated for got justice. Even when it seemed it was inevitable, such as with the murder of Ezell Ford, where the Los Angeles Police Commission ruled that the officers who killed him had violated multiple policies, the local district attorney still refused to press charges. I could hardly believe it. We got close in some cases: in Maryland, the Baltimore state's attorney, a young Black woman named Marilyn Mosby, charged all six officers who were involved in Freddie Gray's death with crimes ranging from reckless endangerment to murder, and the coroner ruled Gray's death a homicide. But yet again, not a single officer in that case was found guilty. It was distressing. The public pursuit of justice had never been this energized in my entire life, but even with that, the system did not budge an inch.

And listen—hear my heart: We were right to march and protest and demonstrate and tweet. We were right to chant

"Black lives matter!" and "I can't breathe!" We were right to raise Black Power fists and wear shirts with the faces and names of victims on them. We were right to do all of that. It forced the entire world to stop and understand the pain and plight of impacted communities, and it generated crucial awareness for a topic that historically had been ignored. But when all was said and done, the Justice Department failed to bring a single civil rights charge against any of these officers, and the White House task force created a strong report but disbanded without any binding actions from the government. For all the hope that hinged on the Obama administration on this issue, the actual results were sparse. And in spite of all of our work in the first few years of the movement, the system mainly resisted our pressure and just shrugged us off.

Part of the reason this seemed so shocking was because of the fun-house mirror that is social media. Social media has a strange way of convincing us that the entire world cares about our cause as much as we do, and that by sharing an article or writing a passionate comment or tweet, we are making real strides in our activism. This is a false perception. We can leverage platforms like Twitter, Facebook, and Instagram for social change, but please remember: that's not their primary purpose. Social media exists to be a vehicle for ads. Period. And while the cultural momentum of those platforms can reward behaviors that get us seen and heard, those behaviors are rarely the same ones that change the world for good.

To fight back against the status quo, we need concerted efforts of changemaking that extend beyond clicking a like button or posting an angry status. I know this might sound ironic coming from me—after all, I'm Mr. Social Media—but these platforms are better used as tools for *awareness* than vehicles for systemic change. Starting a Facebook group or retweeting a woke article or sharing an explanatory video can set the groundwork and create the atmospheric energy that enables change, but this is not a form of organizing. If social media impressions and mentions won elections, Beto O'Rourke would've beaten Ted Cruz the moment Beyoncé started sharing about his campaign, and Andrew Gillum and Stacey Abrams would be sitting governors in their respective home states of Florida and Georgia. O'Rourke, Gillum, and Abrams were all mentioned on social media exponentially more than their opponents. They had the online buzz and energy. But again, online activism is not the same as on-the-ground activism. Social media can be a *part* of an organizing strategy, but it is simply not enough to get us out of the dip.

Our social media timelines are false representations of the world and create a dangerous form of technological bias. The algorithms that build those timelines are among the most coveted and influential codes ever created. They were designed and redesigned and tweaked to produce a version of the world for you that rarely deviates outside the lines of your own norms, standards, and expectations. Never before has it been so easy to assume that we have our finger on the pulse of the people, only to find out how outrageously wrong we were about it all.

This is precisely what happened in the 2016 presidential election. While anti-Trump energy fueled news cycles and social media timelines all across the country and gave tens of millions of people the impression that he was about to be crushed in the election, Trump won thirty states, won the Electoral College by seventy-seven votes, and became president of the United States. The following morning, as I traveled to speak as a guest on the *Ebro in the Morning* show on New York's Hot 97 radio station, I saw people standing on street corners in Manhattan hugging each other and crying. A longtime New Yorker told me that he had not seen so many people so publicly distraught since 9/11. They weren't just upset over Trump's win; they were confronting the harsh reality that they hadn't even considered that such a thing could happen.

When it comes down to it, energy starts movements. It creates awareness, it brings people together, it builds momentum. And the truth is that you will *always* struggle to make change without those things. But energy alone is not enough. Have you ever built a campfire? A match provides energy, but you can throw a lit match at a pile of wood over and over and over again and it will rarely catch fire. You have to set the logs up just right. You have to collect brush and twigs and kindling and position them perfectly underneath. And then, and only then, if all of these factors line up, you can start a campfire with a single match. So it goes with organizing.

What I did not account for in New York, in St. Louis and Ferguson, in Cleveland, in Los Angeles, was that the people in power who made the real decisions on all of these cases were the human equivalent of wet wood. Even as literal buildings burned, as the blood of children and teenagers who had been killed by police flowed down streets and into the soil of public parks, they were not moved. The systems and structures of oppression, and the people who oversee and guide them, are fully willing to wait out the energized masses. They are content to watch our marches and protests from the windows of their offices or on their screens without ever yielding to a single one of our demands. They will stall us and do everything they can to slow our momentum to a snail's pace, in the hope that doing so will mean that we lose steam and give up, keeping the status quo fully intact. They are banking on our collective wave of energy simply being a blip on the radar, something that they can steamroll over or count on dying out over time.

All effective movements begin with highly energized people, but we must be careful not to confuse our most energized moments with change itself. You could have a room of ten energized people or a march of millions and end up with the exact same result if you don't pair that energy with the other steps I will soon outline. Energy is so damn deceiving that way. The chants and outraged op-eds and marching feet of the people can often feel like change, but those actions are just a start.

The truth is that the energy and attention sparked by tragedy are fleeting. The wall-to-wall media coverage and public discussion that result from those events are temporary. They disappear before you know it. But when these moments come, we must be prepared to speak out, and use this critical time to build awareness and momentum for the causes we care about. Because eventually the spotlight will dim and people will move on — and so we must be able to smartly pivot from building awareness about a cause to quickly organizing energized people in meaningful ways that will last far beyond a narrow media window.

Too often, we are highly energized but very loosely organized. Nothing kills the energy of a movement more than poor organization, and nothing sustains and grows a movement from the energy stage to the action stage more than being deeply and strategically organized. I've learned this the hard way. Being aware of a problem and highly energized to change it is not enough. Next, let me unpack and explain for you what it means to be deeply organized for change.

# 8

# Organized People

CHANGE BEGINS WITH PEOPLE. And while people must be highly energized in order to break through the status quo, if they aren't quickly organized in deep, meaningful, practical ways, their energy will soon fade, and what could've blossomed into a movement will dissolve into something much less impactful than that: a moment. And here's the thing: Energized moments are beautiful. They are cathartic and therapeutic. We need them. But their benefit is almost exclusively internal unless the momentum and energy is converted into an organized, cohesive movement for change. In almost every way, we are more energized than we are organized. And that's a recipe for failure. It may be a well-intentioned, good-natured failure, but it's a failure nonetheless. Energized people must organize themselves as if their lives, and the lives of future generations, depend on it. We're not there yet. We're not even close.

To get there, we're going to need a significantly deeper level of organization than most pressing causes and issues currently have. I don't say that as an insult to all of the good people out there putting in such hard work, but as someone whose hands are also in the dirt, and whose heart is just as broken by the state of the world as yours. To get us out of this dip, we need more of us to be deeply focused, moving in the same direction at the same time. And as painful as it may be to hear, what I am about to tell you is equally difficult for me to say: we've been out-organized.

Some could argue that that's an oversimplification of our problems, but the truth is that many of the greatest challenges we face on guns, the environment, mass incarceration, campaign finance, healthcare, white supremacy, education, income inequality, and so much more are a direct result of one side organizing and fighting more effectively for their priorities than the other. I'm not saying they fight fair. I'm not saying they haven't gerrymandered districts in such an obscene way that they become impossible for anybody but ultraconservatives to win. I'm not saying they haven't closed polling sites throughout the country and made it harder for people to a cast their votes. Despicable though they may be, real people organized those underhanded realities into existence—which means that real people can dismantle them, too. But until the quality and scale of our organization drastically improves, we will be more outraged than we are effective. And as long as our outrage outpaces our organization, we will lose way more than we ever win. And for us, those losses aren't a game. When we lose on the issues that we care about, real lives are at stake.

Most leaders I work with would say that the American Civil Rights era was a golden age for organizing. I agree with that, but I've noticed something when we use the Civil Rights movement as a model for how we organize today. Most often, when the movement is commemorated on posters, in commercials, and in social media posts, we are celebrating specific aspects of their organizing: the boycotts, sit-ins, and protests; the March on Washington; the crossing of the Edmund Pettus Bridge in Selma; the work done by the young people who were sprayed with fire hoses that had water pressure so high it could peel off their skin; the work done by those who were harassed and harangued and bitten by police dogs. Those actions were central to the success of the movement, and they should be honored accordingly. But because those particular moments are frequently the only images we see over and over again, we tend to forget about or diminish all of the behind-the-scenes work that went into making those actions possible.

I'd compare the Civil Rights movement to an iceberg. Did you know that 91.7 percent of an iceberg's mass is submerged underwater? The impressive display we see is only a fraction of the whole; the rest is invisible to us. The Civil Rights movement was no different. What happened in the streets, at lunch counters, at marches, and on the mic — of course, all of that was important. But those public expressions all came from a deep, rich, highly relational, even familial network that existed when the cameras were turned off. I call that the invisible Civil Rights movement. Everything that we know and love about the visible movement emerged from that private, relational place. The invisible work happened in church basements and at kitchen tables, in union halls and college classrooms. It was the work of Mississippi sharecroppers planning while they toiled, and the conversations among clusters of friends in their living rooms after the kids went to bed. Thousands upon thousands of strategic planning meetings occurred long before the public actions that we've all come to know so well ever took place. Behind closed doors were brilliant men, women, queers, Quakers, communists, and socialists who were never given the public credit they deserved for the private organizing work they did. Now, of course, they didn't do the work for credit, but their erasure from public history denies us the rich, holistic models for change that we all need to see. They were the foundation of the movement and rarely made it to the microphone or the main stage; invisible but indispensable.

I'm not here to romanticize the Civil Rights movement, either. It was full of dysfunction and dissension. Their work was some of the hardest work done in all of American history, and they faced threats not only from white supremacist violence but from covert government intervention as well. And yet they endured in great part because of the closeness of their bonds and the tightness of their organizing. Our modern movements often struggle because the necessary relationships and philosophies that give movements their depth are missing. While it's better to organize as a bunch of relatively friendly strangers than not organize at all, it'd be way more effective if we did this work as close friends and partners in the struggle. The relational work of a movement is not ancillary, it's vital. And as much as social media is said to have been created to bring people together, it's no substitute for actual human interactions and relationships.

Over the years, I've been able to see tried-and-true methods for organizing that have allowed for these types of meaningful relationships to develop. Let me walk you through some of the most critical points of what it means to be deeply organized.

Every day, the most organized groups and campaigns in the world welcome in new volunteers and donors. It's important that we make these pathways to volunteerism and donating wide and easy to navigate for all of our organizations. By the time somebody signs up to give their time or hard-earned money for a cause, they are already energized for change; this is your opportunity to invite them in further, so you want to make the next steps as clear and as accessible as you can.

In my early organizing days, the conventional wisdom was to try and get a person's first name, last name, mailing address, phone number, and email address. Nowadays, I see most organizations asking for only a first name and an email address. That's one way to gather information, sure. But here's the thing: organizing deeply means making the process *human*. Collecting an email address may allow you to organize widely, in the sense that it helps you to quickly amass a large number of contacts, but it doesn't allow you to organize deeply. Human beings have data points, sure, but when we reduce them *to* data points, we are missing critical opportunities for connection.

The greatest untapped resources in all of organizing are *human* resources. People have skills, passions, and expertise that simply often aren't being utilized in any meaningful way in fighting for a cause. If you have an email list with ten thousand people on it, it's likely that you have volunteers with every possible skill you'd ever need, but our current methods of organizing are not able to identify and maximize those talents.

This is why I'm saying that you need to get to know the people in the movement—really get to know them—as much as you can. An email address tells you nothing about who they are, where they come from, what experiences or skills they have that might be valuable for your work. Once you make the process more human, and dig into the actual lives of the people in your community, the change becomes much more reachable, the strategy richer and more complex. Your volunteers with writing talents could help you spread the message; those who are great in the kitchen can provide meals; those who are data nerds can help you with statistical research. You aren't going to know these things if you don't ask, which is why *effective, active communication* is essential to deep organizing.

Next up, once you have a more realistic sense of the gifts, stories, and skills that exist within your community, it's essential to ask people how many hours per week, or even per day, they are willing to volunteer for the cause. You may have some people who feel like they can handle twenty hours a week, while others flat out tell you that they're slammed and don't have a single moment to spare. That's important to know. Instead of a one-size-fits-all approach to volunteer lists, organizations can classify volunteers according to how much time they have to offer.

The other critical aspect of getting to know your community is related to the idea of building smart, info-rich networks. I recently spoke in Kansas City for the annual gala of an organization called The Help KC. It was founded by Candance Wesson, a brilliant, compassionate soul who served eleven months in federal prison for a first-time, nonviolent tax offense. When Candance was released from prison with a felony on her record, she couldn't find a single place of employment that would hire her. It was then that she decided to build an organization to effectively help women transition out of prison and back into society.

At the gala, I wanted to demonstrate before the audience of nearly six hundred people what it would mean for us to organize deeply to support the work that Candance was doing. In that cavernous ballroom, people were sitting at tables of ten. "I believe one table in this room that is highly energized for change, and deeply organized for it, can accomplish more than all of the other tables in this room combined," I told the room. It's a provocative statement, but it's true. If the other fifty-nine tables of people just walked out of that ballroom at the end of the gala, completely disconnected from one another, unaware of their shared potential and unclear about their mission, they'd accomplish nothing.

From there, I chose one table in the room and asked each person to tell me precisely what skills they could offer Candance's organization. At this one table, we found that there was a caterer, two event planners, an accountant, a high school teacher, a financial adviser, a banker, an elected official, a budding writer, and a seasoned charity executive. Every single one of them had skills that could be useful for the charity we were there to celebrate that night. The charity was nowhere near being in a financial position to hire those ten people to work for them in an official capacity, but each individual, right there on the spot, openly said they'd be willing to donate their time and talent if asked. In that moment, both Candance and her husband leaned over to tell me that just knowing those bits of information immediately stoked ideas for actionable tasks within the organization that these men and women could one day consider doing. If I hadn't paused for a moment to ask about their resources, they would've just remained donors. That's not the worst thing in the world, but by pushing that ask even further, I immediately enhanced the opportunities for growth in this organization and allowed the donors to see themselves as more active participants in the charity. Imagine what would have happened if I'd done that for every table in the room!

Then I pushed this concept a bit further. "Change is not just about *what* you know, it is often about *who* you know," I told the crowd. "If I asked you each to name five people you know personally who you think could help this organization assist women in their transition from prison back to society, could you do it? Take a moment," I said. Each person at the same table reflected, and responded that they did indeed have five friends or associates, from all walks of life, who they thought could be of value in helping this cause. This table of ten people expanded their reach within seconds.

This is what it looks like to organize deeply. It's about understanding the talents and resources of the people who've already made it clear they want to support the cause, and then figuring out how you can empower them to personally invite their most trusted friends along for the journey. It might sound uncomfortable, but sometimes you just have to straight up ask people whom they know and whom they are willing to introduce you to who might be able to support your particular cause. If you skip this step of organizing, meaningful connections are often lost, which means you have also lost a huge potential to effect change.

I'm not saying any of this is easy to manage. It isn't. I tried and failed a few times before I finally figured out how to get it right for my own organizations. Managing highly skilled volunteers, particularly at scale, requires either a full-time staff person, a dedicated, experienced group of committed volunteers, or both. Over time I realized that while I'm great at motivating people to volunteer, I'm not very good at managing them once they make the commitment. I've learned the hard way that once volunteers come through the door, I need a skilled team to pass the baton to. For the two political organizations that I helped found, the Real Justice PAC and the Action PAC, we now have thousands of volunteers who are managed in small groups by other skilled, reliable volunteers who have demonstrated their commitment to our cause. We typically break volunteers into smaller batches of one hundred or even one thousand people, set some very clear goals and guidelines for them, and then let them loose. We have several paid staff members whose job it is to oversee and manage our volunteer leaders. Every organization needs that type of concerted, thoughtful assembly of its members.

People sometimes say that organizing is a marathon, not

a sprint, but I'd mix that up a little: it's equal parts sprint and marathon. On some days I lead teams that are moving full speed ahead, with reckless abandon, to hit urgent, emergency deadlines or goals. That sprint work can happen only in bursts or you'll burn yourself and your team out, but your teams have to be nimble enough to be able to work quickly when needed. Other times we understand that we are working to shift entire systems in ways that won't happen in hours or days, maybe not even in weeks or months, but in *years* of sustained work. Whatever the speed or pace of the work, it's essential to know your limitations and understand when you must surround yourself with people whose strengths and weaknesses complement your own.

What I am about to say is so simple and obvious that it's going to sound stupid. The more I've been an actual part of real, living, breathing communities of change, the more change I've been a part of. A huge part of understanding your role in making change can only happen inside of a community created for the change itself. When you care about an enormous problem in the world but aren't part of a team that is trying its damnedest to tackle it, you can easily feel overwhelmed. Organized people exist to get us unstuck and moving in the right direction.

Maybe you're a natural loner or introvert. I get that. In some ways, I am, too. Social media and technology can allow people like us to exist in an online space without ever making those important human connections offline. I was a hyper-social kid until I got to high school. The harassment and brutality I experienced and all of the time I spent recovering from my surgeries forced me to become a loner. I regularly have to shake that feeling off in order to be able to build the trusting relationships that changemaking requires. But I always feel a gravitational pull back to being a loner. I love people, I truly do, but I could be alone for days on end and feel just fine about it. Movement work requires that I regularly get over myself, and in doing so, I became a part of some of the most impactful movements for change in modern American history. That's what I want for you as well. It may take some searching, and some trial and error, but you need to find your offline, real-life community, plug in, and get to work. Doing so is not only going to make the world a better place, it's going to add depth and meaning to your life that simply could never exist outside of such a community.

When a community or cause is both highly energized and deeply organized, it will have a dramatically greater capacity for impact and change. When these two factors are both present, you will begin to see possibilities for change that simply aren't available in a community that is just energized. But if you take that energized community, organize it, and then add the step I'll discuss next, you will turbocharge the potential for change.

## 9

# Sophisticated Plans

ONCE YOU HAVE A COMMUNITY that is energized and organized, the third element you'll need to make change is a strategic plan. Now, that sounds simple enough, but this plan needs to be as sophisticated, robust, and nuanced as the problems you're trying to solve. You can have some small, meaningful victories here and there without a strategic plan in place, but the impact will be limited. Energized and organized people are a powerful force, but they will be overwhelmed and fall apart without the right plan in place.

While it may sound obvious that you need a serious plan to make change, as I've traveled across the country to speak to people about the problems we're facing, what I've often found is that a huge percentage of well-intentioned, good-hearted activists and organizers are working without a well-conceived plan. Whenever I speak about changemaking to a room full of people, I always begin by asking one simple question. It goes something like this: "Can you unpack for me your plan about how, precisely, you hope to solve the problems that I know you're most deeply concerned about?" I ask it with love, prefacing it by letting the room know that this is a judgment-free zone, but even so, the question itself often makes people uneasy.

Nine times out of ten, when I ask people for their strategy to solve a problem, they respond not by detailing their plans, but by sharing an expert-level understanding of the problem. It makes sense. Most of us know the problems related to the issues we care so much about. We've spent time with them. We've brooded and grieved over them. We've read articles and books and watched videos about them. We can speak extemporaneously about them. The truth is, many activists and organizers know the problems so well because they are a part of the community most affected by them. But while knowing a problem, and knowing it intimately, can and should *inform* our best plans, the problem and the plan are just not one and the same.

The forces that we are up against aren't just fierce; they are complicated, well fortified, and deeply entrenched. We may be facing a modern incarnation of the problem, but often these issues have deep, twisted roots that meander across all fifty states and hundreds if not thousands of laws and corporations. And what I've seen happen more times than I can count is that the sheer size and scale of these problems bulldozes over our itty-bitty, on-the-fly plans. Until we create plans that honestly, earnestly acknowledge the depth and complexity of what we're up against, they will fail—we will fail—no matter how energized or organized we are. If we go to battle with the wrong plan of attack, we lose. It's that simple.

I was already a pastor when I went to seminary at Candler School of Theology at Emory University, in Atlanta. There, I had a professor named Dr. Tom Long, a brilliant man once recognized as one of the twelve most effective preachers in the English-speaking world. Dr. Long was a genial, kind soul, as well as a gifted wordsmith. Unlike most of my classmates, I was already leading a church and had been preaching for over a decade. I was looking forward to learning from Dr. Long, but in a way, I arrogantly thought I didn't really need the class, given my previous experience.

After I finished preaching my first sermon in front of Dr. Long and my classmates, I was reasonably confident that it was A-grade material. I had clearly held their attention and had made some points that landed. Dr. Long smiled at me warmly, as was his way, and then proceeded to give some feedback. "Shaun—you set up the text masterfully. It was captivating and interesting and got my attention right out of the gate." I nodded, pleased with this initial assessment. "Everything after that, though, was just pretty good," he continued, in his slight southern drawl.

Dr. Long then offered me a critical piece of advice, something that has stuck with me ever since. He walked up to the whiteboard and proceeded to draw a very small house. "Shaun, that house represents the body and conclusion of your sermon." Attached to the house, in front of it, he began drawing an enormous rectangular platform that was probably twenty times larger than the house. It took up almost the entire whiteboard. In the middle of the massive rectangle, Dr. Long then wrote these words: FRONT PORCH.

"And this," Dr. Long continued, "this enormous porch, represents the introduction to your sermon. It was big and beautiful, but Shaun, I'm afraid you built an enormous porch for a tiny house," he said, hammering my ego back down to earth with the sweetness of caramel. We smiled at each other. He had nailed it. The structure of my sermon was a direct reflection of my preparation. I had spent hours and hours working on the introduction of that talk and ended up rushing the body and the conclusion as I ran out of prep time. And when I preached it, he could tell. You couldn't fool him.

That's what I see when I ask people to tell me all about their strategic plans to solve the problems that keep them up at night. They build a huge porch with a tiny house. And don't get me wrong: that huge porch is masterfully done; it's made up of layers and layers of analysis of all that is wrong and broken in society. But without taking that information and contextualizing it with an eye toward nuanced, sophisticated action-plan development, we'll never get as far as we need to go. If we are energized and organized, and we have a half-baked plan, no amount of energy or organization can make up for that plan. It will fall apart. That sermon I preached in class had a great introduction, but the body needed a lot of work, and so do our plans. We may have nailed the intro, but it's time to get to work on everything else.

For most of my organizing life, dating all the way back

to my time as student government president at Morehouse in 1999, I've brought energized and organized people to the table, but I've often failed to operate from a well-conceived plan. I've believed that I could dive headfirst into a crisis with a mix of charisma, confidence, and my public speaking skills and connect with highly energized people who were super-charged for change. In some ways, that *was* enough to get me through the front door, and it could often sustain our work for a few weeks, or even a few months, but the longer we operated without a strategic plan, just running off of my instincts, the less effective we became.

Never was that more apparent than during the first year I spent organizing relief and aid to Haiti in the immediate aftermath of the devastating 2009 earthquake. First, I need to take you all the way back to that winter, when I was the lead pastor at a new church in Atlanta called the Courageous Church. Our church was planning a trip to Haiti. It would be our first international trip, and we were thinking through smart ways to partner with organizations and people on the ground there. Twitter was still relatively new, but I used it to connect to several grassroots leaders in Port-au-Prince to try and help me understand the people and culture better.

On a random Tuesday afternoon that January, I was scrolling through my Twitter feed and started seeing a barrage of tweets and retweets from the young Haitian leaders I followed. One of the most devastating earthquakes in modern history had just struck the island, and their tweets were providing real-time updates about the devastation and urgency of the crisis. I turned on the TV: no one was covering it yet, but the tweets kept coming in. It was overwhelming. At that time, no natural disaster had ever unfolded like that on social media before.

In the years leading up to this, I had gotten accustomed to using social media to rally people for social good. Just three months prior, I had organized thousands of volunteers to help families in the suburban town of Austell, Georgia, when entire neighborhoods were submerged underwater during a historic flood. Nine months before that, I had been featured on the *Today* show and the local news in Atlanta for using Twitter and Facebook to raise money to purchase new school uniforms and Christmas toys for every child at Frank L. Stanton Elementary School. Facebook had covered my work on its official blog, which was a big deal back then, and people started calling me the Facebook Pastor. So I knew a few things about how to leverage the internet to help people in need, but this? This was on another level.

We didn't know it yet, but the Haitian government would eventually announce that over 300,000 people died in the earthquake, many of them trapped under enormous mounds of rubble. The earth shook so violently that at least 150,000 homes and more than 30,000 businesses were completely destroyed. A staggering 300,000 people were injured, and over 1.5 million people were instantly homeless. The nation was left with nearly no electricity. Most hospitals were critically damaged, and even if they hadn't been so badly damaged, there was nowhere near enough capacity to respond to this level of human need. These numbers on a page can hardly do justice to the sheer size and scope and depth of the trauma and damage, but let me give you this point of comparison: the American Civil War was the deadliest war in American history, and the death and injury toll experienced in Haiti in just *one day* was equivalent to the number of casualties in one year of that war.

Sensing the urgency of the situation, I immediately reached out to those young leaders in Haiti—brave men like Carel Pedre and Karl Jean-Jeune—and asked how a guy like me could help. None of us understood the magnitude of what they were facing just yet, but when they asked for GPS devices and high-powered military-grade laptops with satellite services built in so that they could assist efforts to locate survivors, I jumped at the opportunity to make it happen. That day, I tweeted about the need to my audience, we raised the money, and forty-eight hours later, I figured out a back channel to get the equipment to them.

Ushahidi, an online crisis-mapping team based at Tufts University, got to work within two hours of the earthquake. When I could, I'd feed them information that people started sending me once they saw that I was dedicated to helping. The volume of information was staggering. Then I started working around the clock, building teams of online volunteers to scour by collecting their data through contact forms and emailing and texting out tasks as they came to me. They would scan social media for the locations of people who tweeted that they needed help, find out precisely what needs people had at each location, and then pass that information on to Ushahidi or other volunteer teams we connected with on the ground in Haiti. We were all winging it, but we knew that every hour mattered. At that point, I was so desperate to help save lives that the idea of pausing to create a plan seemed ludicrous to me.

Some of the smartest, most compassionate people I had ever met jumped in to help. While Haiti's main airport in Port-au-Prince was closed to commercial flights, emergency responders flew to the Dominican Republic and then drove across the border to Haiti from there. Others figured out that they could charter small private planes to various tiny landing strips around the country. A buddy of mine, a country pastor from the hills of North Carolina named Mark Hunnicutt, showed up in Haiti on a rescue mission with several of his friends. Using GPS coordinates given to me by friends on the ground in Haiti, I guided them on where to go and what to do from my living room. Later, I found myself on the phone with Republican senator Bill Frist—a surgeon by training who ended up in Haiti less than twenty-four hours after the earthquake—and communicated to him some of the places in greatest need. CNN's Dr. Sanjay Gupta was there and said that the island had an urgent need for neurosurgeons, so I put out the call on social media. It was a nonstop effort. I was barely sleeping. And the results were still devastating. We cried way more than we cheered. I regularly helped guide people on missions where they could hear what they thought were survivors under rubble whom they just could not get to because of the massive wreckage. Other times, I directed rescuers to locations where people insisted that their families were trapped—only to have the team arrive there and learn that nobody on earth could've survived such devastation.

With every day that passed, it became clearer that people were desperate for some type of temporary housing. Hundreds of thousands of people had no shelter from the rain, no cover from the sun, and nowhere to sleep at night. And so local Haitians on the ground, seeing that I had been able to successfully send gear and coordinate volunteers, asked if I could begin sending tents.

Without any consideration of what that would look like, I agreed to begin the work, and dove headfirst into it. I didn't pause for a moment to craft even a *sketch* of a plan. I didn't consider the challenges or the consequences; I didn't think about what the next phase was going to be after getting the tents there. I didn't even consider step two, and I damn sure didn't consider steps nine or ten. I just knew that I was asked to help, and I started running full speed ahead.

On the same day I was asked to start sending tents, I created a wish list on Amazon containing every single tent that the site sold for people to purchase. I listed the shipping address as the address for our church offices, without any thought to where we'd store them or sort them once they arrived. By the end of the first day, thousands of tents had been purchased from our wish list and sent to our offices. By the end of the first week, we had surpassed nearly 25,000 tents. By the end of the first month, tentmakers like Coleman were sending us pallets upon pallets of tents. The actress Eva Longoria even came on board to be the spokesperson for our efforts.

As the donations from generous people all over the country continued to roll in, our offices were stacked floor to ceiling with tents, packed so tight that our staff and volunteers could hardly get in and out. Our efforts started to overwhelm the local mail services, with the shipments filling multiple full-size trucks every day. Once relief supplies reached Haiti, the processing of the shipping containers became the Wild West. Getting something successfully shipped, received, and transported to its intended recipient was nearly impossible, so we operated on the fly. Friends in Haiti coached us. We bribed people. We sent armed convoys. We stuffed private jets with tents and had Haitians meet them with trucks on the runway and take them from there. We sent them on cruise ships. We sent them through the Dominican Republic. On more than one occasion, thousands of the tents we'd sent were taken by force. People were desperate. We didn't care that they were taken from us, just as long as nobody got hurt in the process.

When I finally traveled to Haiti the next month, I saw our tents being used all over the country. It was unbelievable to see row upon row of them being put to good use. And I was proud, too. It was the hardest thing I'd ever done in my life, an around-the-clock operation with little structural support and the highest of stakes.

But over time, I noticed something troubling. When we sent those tents, they were meant to be used for a few weeks, maybe a few months. But every time I'd visit Haiti or send teams, we noticed that the tent cities were growing bigger and bigger. Six months after the hurricane, our tents were still there, faded by the scorching tropical sun, tattered by the wind, and often patched together with duct tape. A year later, the tents continued to serve as the primary shelter for thousands of people. It was maddening. I'd like to say that "this was not our plan," but we didn't have a plan. The tents were intended to serve as a temporary Band-Aid, not a housing solution. We had assumed that a bigger, broader housing strategy would soon be executed; after all, more than $13.6 billion in aid had been given. That was enough to rebuild hundreds of thousands of homes, but as time ticked by, we never saw that new construction happen. The American Red Cross alone received nearly $500 million in donations but ended up building just six homes—yes, *six*—in total.

My expectation was that our tents would be a step toward something much more substantial—new roads, new homes, new schools, new communities. They weren't. I'm disgusted even thinking about it.

With the best of intentions, we sent people temporary shelters designed to get them through that first spring or summer, never imagining that they'd be in use years later, and that billions of dollars in aid would be squandered and unaccounted for along the way. It's not that I had the ability to predict what was to come, but I wasn't even thinking a few steps ahead. Our efforts weren't a failure, but over time, they felt damn near close to one. Had I understood that our tents were going to be used for years, I would've planned the entire project differently. I would've asked people to send industrial-strength military tents designed to withstand the elements, or I would've skipped the tents and started a housing program from the get-go where we worked with local builders and contractors in Port-au-Prince to construct one home at a time. But that's the point—I didn't have a plan. I didn't consider any long-term implications; I just acted in the moment. I was flying by the seat of my pants, coordinating most of these operations from my laptop and BlackBerry (the iPhone before we had iPhones, for all you young'uns) and operating from a "by any means necessary" philosophy, as so many other organizations appeared to be dragging their feet. We were energized and organized and we got stuff done, but a plan would have made us so much more effective in the long term.

Everything my community and I did in Haiti, we did with our whole hearts and maximum effort. But because I didn't operate with a strategic plan and just freestyled everything, we missed out on opportunities to do work that would have had a lasting impact. In the aftermath of a natural disaster or an act of violence, it's hard as hell to be able to think clearly enough to build a strategic plan. Imagine for a moment that your house was on fire. What would you do if someone asked you to craft a thoughtful strategic plan to get your loved ones to safety while your house was engulfed in flames? That's what it often feels like for so many people doing frontline organizing. It's hard to see the big picture, but it has to be done—even if that means finding people who aren't necessarily right in the middle of the battle who can partner with you to help create a plan.

In 2016, I joined a local coalition of New Yorkers who not only were energized and organized, but had the most thoughtful strategic plan to confront youth incarceration that I had ever seen. It was called the Raise the Age coalition, and it was designed specifically to raise the minimum age of prosecution for children. Doing so, we believed, would help interrupt the school-to-prison pipeline. Seeing how the organization strategized helped me to understand the value of collaboration, communication, and nuanced, sophisticated goal setting. It completely changed the way I view organizing.

Through the 1980s and early 1990s, as the so-called war on drugs continued with the Reagan, Bush, and Clinton administrations, mass incarceration exploded, surpassing one million people behind bars for the very first time, then blowing right past two million people by 2001. To reach those numbers, one of the most nefarious policies introduced during that time was that states started arresting and charging children as adults. At first, states across the country began lowering the age to include seventeen-year-olds, then sixteen-year-olds. It was unconscionable, and when we thought it couldn't get any worse, states from coast to coast started charging kids as young as fifteen as adults, then fourteen, and even thirteen. South Carolina charged and convicted a twelve-year-old boy named Christopher Pittman as an adult for committing murder. Pennsylvania then charged an eleven-year-old boy named Jordan Brown as an adult for committing murder; even more tragically, he was later exonerated for the crime. It was fundamentally absurd. In fact, thirteen states don't have any minimum age at all for prosecuting children as adults and sending them to adult jails and prisons for committing violent crimes.

By 2016, many states had reformed their laws so that minors could be charged as adults only for the most violent crimes, but two states held out, continuing to automatically charge all children older than fifteen as adults no matter the offense. In other words, in these two states, if a sixteen-year-old kid stole a candy bar from a convenience store, the child was automatically charged as an adult and could be sent to a jail housing adults. The first state didn't surprise me so much—that was North Carolina—but the second one did. It was New York.

When I first moved to New York, back in 2016, to work for the *Daily News*, I had some assumptions about the state that just weren't true. I couldn't rationalize how a place that I had long viewed as a bastion of progressive politics could also be one of the last two states in the nation to automatically prosecute children as adults for all crimes. What I quickly learned was that while New York State does indeed have some loud progressive pockets, it can be much more moderate than most outsiders believe. For nearly ten years before I moved there, activists had been fighting hard to raise the minimum age of prosecutable crimes in the state. They had poured their hearts into the cause, but no matter what they did, the law remained, and New York's jails and prisons continued to be full of children forced into some of the worst conditions imaginable.

Then, finally, an alliance of more than a hundred groups, leaders, and organizations called Raise the Age was formed. What that coalition was able to achieve in twelve months blew my mind. Previously, dozens of the groups within the coalition had valiantly fought to raise the minimum age for incarceration, but they weren't fighting together in ways that complemented one another's strengths and weaknesses. Instead of one unified fight, it was dozens of well-intentioned but isolated battles that built awareness but not change. Their efforts no doubt loosened the lid on the jar of change, but the coalition blew the lid off.

At the time, I was leading a stealth group of more than

100,000 online volunteers from all fifty states and over one hundred countries, called the Injustice Boycott. It was the only group of its kind—one whose actions were focused primarily on digital organizing, social media, and the smart use of technology—working within the coalition. As a first step, our team created a social media directory of all the organizations in the coalition and worked to increase the following of every group by as much as 500 percent. Many of the organizations were doing brilliant work and had smart content to share about Raise the Age, but they were often broadcasting it to the online equivalent of an empty auditorium—so they welcomed the newfound audience we provided. Boosting their following also engendered immediate goodwill among groups that otherwise might have been skeptical of my presence. Many of them had been working on this cause for years and didn't know me well. Daily, sometimes several times a day, I'd send action steps to our volunteers to write or amplify targeted tweets and Facebook posts. Doing so made Raise the Age trend on Twitter for the very first time. My team would make tens of thousands of phone calls to public officials asking them to support the legislation, and send just as many personal emails lobbying for it. It was a beautiful thing and added a real sense of momentum and energy to the cause. A year later I would learn that Heather Heyer, who was murdered by a white supremacist in Charlottesville, had been one of the active volunteers for our cause, regularly sharing our posts and making calls.

Of the hundred-plus organizations in the Raise the Age coalition, I'd estimate that at least half of them had never been in the same room with one another before. I'd go so far as to say that the majority of us didn't know that most of the other groups in the coalition even *existed*. At least a third of the groups were some of the oldest, most established and respected charities for children in New York. There were scholarly organizations rooted in academic research, and professional organizations made up of doctors, lawyers, and teachers. Groups from every faith background and from every region of the state were represented. Both old-school and new-school civil rights organizations were in the coalition, bringing their unique perspectives to the table. In total, the massive union that made up Raise the Age represented countless New Yorkers of every age, hue, race, gender, nationality, culture, religion, ability, sexual orientation, income level, education, profession, perspective, and style. I had never seen anything like it.

The breadth and depth of this coalition allowed the problem to be approached from every angle imaginable. Doctors provided brain scans and medical case studies. Scholars provided exhaustive source documents and academic position papers. Religious leaders brought sacred texts and moral arguments. Activists brought not only passion and urgency, but the painful stories of people and families impacted by the draconian law. Experienced, ethical lobbyists were hired to help the coalition navigate the complicated political terrain. A world-class PR and communications firm was brought on board by the coalition leaders to help them nail down their media strategy. And respected foundations were recruited to provide essential financial support for the work. Forming the coalition allowed every organization—

and every staffer and volunteer working within those organizations—to focus on what they do best instead of stretch-
ing themselves thin by attempting to play every role in the
process of change.

Perhaps the single most important and effective part of
the Raise the Age coalition was divvying up the responsibilities for influencing New York's governor, Andrew Cuomo,
to endorse, support, and eventually sign new legislation to
raise the age of criminal responsibility to eighteen. Each organization and member of the coalition was asked to play
a very particular, sometimes shocking role in the name of
change. It was genius. Some of the organizations and leaders would overtly support Cuomo throughout the entire
process. They were assigned to be at his side and in his ear,
to be friends and allies. And in doing so, they gained his
trust and the trust of his team. In the middle of our campaign for Raise the Age, those allies of Cuomo hosted a
justice reform event in which he was the keynote speaker.
This was definitely strategic. See, at that time, Governor
Cuomo was still mulling a run for president of the United
States, and the coalition understood that he'd relish the opportunity to look like a hero in his home state. The goal of
that event was to get Cuomo to publicly commit to supporting Raise the Age—and he ended up doing just that.
He pledged, in an unmistakably clear way, that he would
give the legislation his full support and that he wouldn't
sign a budget without it. The crowd, populated by so many
members of our coalition who were asked to support him
through the process, cheered him as if he had just won reelection.

I wasn't invited to that event, or to any events with Cuomo, for that matter. My job within the coalition had an entirely different purpose. I wasn't asked to be an ally of Cuomo's; I was asked by coalition leaders to be a perpetual thorn in his side. Now, to be clear, I'm good at being a hammer. And I was expected to hammer Governor Cuomo every chance I got—at live events, in emails, all over social media—pushing the idea that he was all talk and no action. I was over-the-top with it. Daily, I would tag him on social media posts and say how I thought it would end his political career if he didn't deliver on his promise. I'd say how I thought he was lying to all of us and that he was never going to support the law. I'd constantly comment that I thought he wasn't really progressive. And while I did all of this, I was keenly aware that playing this particular role probably meant I could never be friends with the man or, really, even set foot in the same room with him. I was relentless, but I did this with intention. Cuomo had proven previously that he had to be damn near bullied into doing progressive work. It was my job to be so persistent and harsh and unmistakably clear about the political consequences of failing to pass this legislation that his team would be motivated to pass it just to prove to the world that people like me, the doubters, were wrong.

At a different point in my life, I would've been too short-sighted to fully appreciate the complexity of this type of approach. The mere notion of Governor Cuomo being the featured guest speaker at a criminal justice reform event would've sent me spinning. But our goal wasn't to be pleased with ourselves; our goal was to carry out our plan to get the law changed, by any means necessary. I never could've played that ally role authentically, and most of the people whose job it was to be Cuomo's sympathetic buddy never could've played mine. But because we all operated from a strategic plan and understood that each role was critically important to its success, it was palatable. Having the plan and the coalition in place allowed groups that normally would've been judgmental of one another to put aside their differences in style and come together for the greater good. Without that plan, we might have been at one another's throats.

Watching this in action was a beautiful thing. Old-school organizations like the Citizens' Committee for Children of New York, which had been fighting for New York's children since World War II, were suddenly collaborating with grassroots activists from relatively new organizations known for their radical grassroots work, like the Justice League NYC. This work continued for months and months on end — every day, seven days a week, around the clock, for damn near a year. Initially, after that public declaration of support, we were reasonably confident that Cuomo would sign the bill if it passed the legislature, but then some unexpected political maneuvering shook that certainty. Cuomo had curried favor with a small group of Democrats who were consistently siding with Republicans in the State Senate, and we soon realized that without the support of that faction, we wouldn't have enough votes to pass the legislation. So my team continued to hammer him, and the other Democrats, relentlessly for months, by phone and email and across social media.

Day in and day out, we gave our online volunteers practical action steps. We called the offices of legislators by the thousands. We emailed them until their servers crashed. We took them to task on social media. We made videos and op-eds from the coalition go viral. And while I helped to lead those efforts, all of the other organizations in the coalition were approaching the problem from their own unique angles and perspectives. In other words, we pushed for change from every possible direction.

After months of nonstop campaigning for Raise the Age, the bill finally passed the legislature and was signed by the governor in April of 2017, becoming law at the start of 2018. While it easily passed in the more liberal New York State Assembly, it barely squeaked by in the State Senate. Sit with that for a minute: with all of that effort, all of that energy — with more than one hundred organizations collaborating at once to get the legislation passed — we still *barely* got it done. That's how difficult it is to make real, substantive, systemic change in this nation.

What Governor Cuomo eventually signed into law in the spring of 2017 was not nearly as strong as our original bill, but it represented about 75 percent of what we'd hoped for. Tens of thousands of children would be positively impacted every single year as a result. We'd changed the system. And up to that point, this was the single hardest, most complex, successful campaign I had ever been a part of. Our hard-fought victory hardly made the news in New York and was practically invisible outside of the state, but those of us who had done the work knew that we had fought for and won something that truly mattered. The law is now in full effect and has drastically changed the treatment of kids in New

York's justice system. Thankfully, in 2019, North Carolina followed New York and became the final state in the country to Raise the Age.

Everything we did in the Raise the Age coalition can be duplicated in your city or state for your cause. When we are fighting for change, we have to look beyond more than the current moment, and that's why thinking about the long game and developing a strategic plan is so critical. I'm not trying to discourage any of you from being spontaneously generous; the world needs more of that. But we have to begin accepting the difficult truth that our well-intentioned spontaneous generosity rarely shifts systems. It helps in the moment — and the moments matter — but our short bursts of good deeds aren't making the tangible, measurable, sustainable change that we all want to see. It's good to give a homeless man a few dollars or a warm meal, but it's better to be working on a plan to end homelessness. It's fine to vent on social media about your frustrations concerning police brutality and mass incarceration, but it's a vast improvement to figure out how to actually abolish those systems and replace them with something much better. Without that sort of macro-level consideration, we're bringing forks to soup-eating contests.

The people fighting for change — I'm talking about the ones on the front lines, either leading protests or responding to crises — rarely have the time, space, or emotional bandwidth to craft plans. Ironically, I think they are often the right people to craft those plans, in the sense that they are often the ones with the most expertise about the problems and systems they are confronting. But it's damn near impossible to be consistently fighting on the front lines and designing the plans we need to guide us in our struggles. That's why, for so many generations, the long, deep, hardcore strategic planning—the kind that takes months or even years of full-time work to accomplish—has happened primarily in communities of privilege, from megacorporations to well-funded think tanks and academic centers. Even if we are not funded like these institutions, we have to strategize like them. We cannot continue to count on the same people to run from crisis to crisis and also create plans that will have resounding effects. It hasn't worked historically, and it will not work going forward. As a result, some of us are going to have to break away from the front lines so that we can build teams to craft plans that will change this world. Doing so seems unthinkable to most activists and organizers I know—not just because we are addicted to the life we lead, though that's part of it, but because we know that each and every body is needed on the front lines. I understand that feeling. I battle it myself daily. But the truth is that if we're going to develop new policies and plans and strategies to solve the problems we care about, we can't do that while remaining in the role of first responder.

Well-crafted plans for social change give us the ability to move at a pace, and to go a distance, that we simply would never achieve without them. Every good idea, strategy, and plan needs to be thoughtfully developed. Your plans for change need serious work and consideration. They shouldn't be able to fit on the back of a napkin. They shouldn't be a few bullet points on a web page. These plans need to be robust and thorough, with an eye toward measurable outcomes. At the very least, a plan should resemble the best term paper of your life, with research, evaluation, and clarity at the forefront. It should take you weeks or months, or even longer, to craft. It can be a living document that evolves and changes and grows over time, but you need to give yourself a due date for its completion and get to work. In fact, until you make the time to sketch out your ideas for change, form them into a plan, and begin sharing it privately with people for thoughts and feedback, the plan that exists only in your mind will simply be too fragile to be effective in this rough climate we are in.

If crafting your plan can be a collaborative process with a diverse set of stakeholders at the table, that's going to make the final product superior to anything you could ever develop on your own. You don't have to have a group as large as our Raise the Age coalition, but aim to bring together as many deeply committed groups and leaders as you can. The plan might have only one or two primary authors, but it needs to have serious input from an eclectic mix of people. I was part of the team that wrote and edited the criminal justice reform plan for Bernie Sanders, and that process further clarified for me the importance of sophisticated strategy building. We studied every plan from every other presidential campaign, past and present, and brought in a team of powerful experts, scholars, civil rights leaders, and policy makers to craft and refine the plan over the course of months. Even after it was drafted, we reviewed, debated, and discussed every element of it over and over again. We brought in experts from other fields who had already been through a similar process in creating plans of their own, essentially to kick the tires and look under the hood of what we'd created. And, no doubt, they found flaws that spurred us to revise and hone the plan, so that by the time we released it, it had been through a gauntlet of fact-checkers and editors and revisers. In the end, we created something that not only we could stand by but that could withstand real scrutiny. We created a plan that was a match for the size and scope of the problems we aimed to solve.

A critical aspect of plan development is finding a way to make your message clear and easy to access. You may ultimately opt to have an exhaustive internal plan that guides you and the team, and you could always make that plan publicly available for download. But in doing this, you also have to find a way to condense a full-scale plan into something that is easy for others to understand and remember. Your best plans are only as effective as the ability of everyday people to repeat them back to you. How can they fight for change if they don't really understand the basic goals you hope to achieve and how you hope to accomplish them?

Plans give us the gift of longevity. They take us out of the daily churn of headlines and allow us to use our imaginations to craft a better, more just vision for our world. They give us hope and help us endure the inevitable tragedies and setbacks that are sure to come. They allow us to ponder and pray and consider. They allow us to revise and improve. Plans allow us to seek input and collaboration from others who may see the world and its problems very differently than we do—and sometimes it's that type of collaboration that can open doors. It's not enough for us to be good, to be right, to be moral, to be outraged. Let's be all of those things. But what we're up against is going to require us to also have a strategic plan for victory. We can be good, right, and moral and still lose the most important battles of our lives. Until we bring the full weight of our energy, our organization, and our plans to bear, all at the same time, moving in the same direction, we are just treading water. But it doesn't have to be that way. We are not destined to lose, dammit. We can have a real say in building our future.

*Part Four*

# Stay Human

WHEN I WAS A kid, all I ever wanted to be was an adult, but now that I am one, and I see how hard it truly is, it makes me miss being a little boy. Ignorance was bliss. On some days, particularly the most brutal ones, my wife and I will look at each other and say, "Hard day." Then one of us will reply, "Hard week." Then the other will reply, "Hard month." And we'll keep going back and forth until we eventually end up saying, in unison, "Hard life." And it's true: it's a hard-knock life. The world is full of beauty, but the ugliness and pain can cut so damn deep. And that's without being an activist or fighting for a cause! The default settings for this world are hard to handle.

For me, I find fighting to make change cathartic and therapeutic. I couldn't live in this cruel place and not try to help lift people up, to defend and protect the vulnerable among us. But the truth is, the work of making change is fraught with so many challenges that I regularly see genuinely good people tap out and go in a different direction with their lives. For the first few years, when my own family sometimes asked me to do that very thing, I couldn't imagine it, but now I get it. It's all so hard that I sometimes dream of moving away to a quiet place with them, to never be heard from again. This work can do that to you.

In these final chapters, I want to share my heart with you on the pain and consequences of making public mistakes and how to recover and rebound from them. I want to discuss the reality of burnout and the importance of self-care. And, ultimately, I want to close with the toughest, most important lesson I've learned in my life as an organizer and activist. Because without acknowledging the struggles and learning how to rebound from them, you'll never find your greatest victories.

# 10

# Mistakes and Rebounding from Failure

SINCE THE START of the Black Lives Matter movement, I've advocated for hundreds of families impacted by police violence and bigotry. I've helped to track down, catch, and jail white supremacists. I've written nearly 1,500 articles about injustice. And I've traveled far and wide to motivate people to fight for change in the world. I've always prided myself on being in the fight, in the struggle, working to make a difference. But in all of that work, I've made *so* many mistakes. Some of them were due to inexperience, others from simply being overwhelmed and taking on too much, and yet others from a dangerous mix of arrogance and ego.

If you don't learn from your mistakes, they will take you out. They will cause you and the people around you real harm, and they'll damage or impede the causes you aim to help. I'd like to think that I've squeezed lemonade out of all of the sour lessons I've learned across the years, and that you will be able to learn a few of those lessons now without making the same mistakes I made. But I'm skeptical. People most often learn by trial and error. Athletes need to be in the game. Musicians need to play in front of a crowd. And in order for you to get better at making the world a better place, you need to be out there in the world fighting to make it a better place, and that means you will likely stumble along the way.

We love to romanticize the most impactful movements of the past, in part because history has often smoothed out the rough edges of their mistakes. But you can't name a revolution or a revolutionary that didn't have real struggles or flaws. It comes with the territory. The key is to learn from your mistakes, forgive yourself and forgive others, and bounce back and change course where you need to, because the world needs you!

After fighting against police brutality around the clock for three years and experiencing so many painful losses, I hit a real wall in 2017 and determined that I was going to have to shift gears in how I fought for justice and change moving forward. In the shadow of those losses, I watched as two of my friends from the Bernie Sanders campaign, Becky Bond and Zack Malitz, pivoted in their own changemaking strategies. Becky and Zack were in high demand for their organizing expertise and were courted by multiple campaigns, but they ultimately decided to dedicate themselves to fighting the system in a bold new way. Together, in late 2016, they formed a political organization called Real Justice, which was focused on helping to elect compassionate, accessible, reform-minded district attorneys throughout the country, shaking up the political establishment exactly where it was needed: at the local level.

District attorneys are the primary gatekeepers and puppet masters of America's justice system. They are the central decision-makers who determine the focus, tone, and tenor of how justice operates in the nation's cities and counties. The DAs decide who's prosecuted and how harshly, they can close cases and drop charges, they can force plea deals, and, more than anyone else, they have the power to hold brutal and corrupt police accountable. Of the 10.5 million people arrested in this country every year, the vast majority of their cases come through the office of the local DA, meaning that, by and large, it's the policies of our district attorneys that have helped to construct the most glaring aspects of mass incarceration. But the average American can't even name their local district attorney, let alone describe the role and responsibilities of that position. And most local prosecutors want it that way. As long as they function with relative anonymity, they can continue to perpetuate the same racist, unjust policies that have ruled the system for centuries. Of this nation's 2,437 district attorneys, 95 percent are white and 83 percent are male — which, clearly, does not reflect the diversity of our nation's population. Real Justice's mission was to challenge the worst DAs in the country and replace them with compassionate new ones who were deeply committed to changing the system from the inside out.

Here's what's particularly powerful about their decision to do that. While the United States has thousands of civil rights organizations that understand the value of electing humane DAs, most are banned from even suggesting whom to vote for in these elections. That's because these organizations are generally nonprofit, tax-exempt 501(c)(3)s, which by law prohibits them from being overtly political. They can't endorse political campaigns or coordinate directly with candidates, and they are frequently prohibited from fighting for or against specific ballot initiatives and policies that are up for vote. The same thing applies to churches, schools, fraternities, sororities, and virtually every other group deeply valued by progressive people. And do you know who suffers the most as a result of this? Marginalized people and communities. Virtually every person and organization of influence that speaks to everyday Black Americans is banned from telling those same folks anything of substance about the local elections that will impact them the most. And so the Real Justice PAC was formed to do what so many of our nation's best civil rights organizations and leaders simply aren't allowed to do—get granular about the problems within the legal system, and advocate for solutions directly to the public.

In many ways, the city of Philadelphia became ground zero for justice reform in the United States, because it had the highest rates of incarceration and supervision of any large city in the country. Here's how bad it was: in 2017, after two years of serious citywide reforms and policy changes, the number of people in jail in Philadelphia plummeted by 20 percent—and even after that, it still remained the most incarcerated large city in the nation. With a grassroots movement for change already in place, and an eclectic mix of locally elected officials committed to going all in on reform, Philadelphia became the first city where Real Justice would work to help elect a new district attorney. Like our efforts to pass the Raise the Age legislation in New York, working to elect a bold, change-centered DA in Philadelphia was going to require all hands on deck, with everybody moving in the same direction at the same time on the same message.

Larry Krasner had been a respected civil rights and defense attorney in Philadelphia for nearly twenty years before activists and organizers began recruiting him to run for district attorney. As the local attorney for the Black Lives Matter movement in Philly, Krasner never imagined he'd be asked to take on this role — running the very system he had so often fought against. A bespectacled, middle-aged, gray-haired white man whose vibe was more nerd than freedom fighter, Larry Krasner became a cult hero in the national justice reform community within months of announcing his campaign. He was not only highly informed, but he was unshakable in his determination to radically change the system from the inside out. Upon hearing him speak just one time, I knew he would be a relentless change agent if we could get him elected.

By the time Becky and Zack started Real Justice, I had become of one of the most visible and widely shared voice for justice reform in the country. My social media posts, articles, and fundraisers for families impacted by police violence routinely influenced news cycles and regularly went viral. From time to time, Becky, Zack, and local leaders in Philadelphia asked me to post about Larry's campaign on social media, fundraise for him online, and mention his candidacy as I traveled across the country. As I did so, and as I began sensing that Larry could actually win in Philadelphia, my hope began to be renewed. After years of losing almost every fight for justice against police brutality, the possibility of winning one of these battles finally seemed within reach.

The more Larry campaigned, the more he resonated not just with local voters but with justice reformers and abolitionists all across the country. He is so sincere and believable that it is somewhat disarming; people just weren't used to this level of no-nonsense directness and honesty from a politician. And after being called "completely unelectable" by his critics, in May of 2017, in a crowded seven-way race, Krasner won the Democratic primary by a staggering 17 percent before going on to win the general election against his Republican opponent by a whopping 40 percent that November. And just like that, a committed change agent was now given the keys to the local justice system, to manage and shape it as he saw fit. This was the embodiment of the very mission of Real Justice — to change the justice system from the inside out, city by city, throughout the country.

Right away, Krasner started changing the game. Soon after he took office in January, he fired corrupt prosecutors and published what's called a do-not-call list of corrupt cops whom he stated he would never call to testify again. They had all been found guilty of gross misconduct and violation of various police department policies but were allowed to continue in their positions. And in a bold memo Krasner released the following month, he announced dozens of sweeping reforms to change long-standing policies on cash bail, drug rehabilitation, over-sentencing, and so much more. In an instant, he demonstrated for the rest of the nation everything we hoped and believed DAs could do if they just had the political courage to follow through on their promises.

For me, his victory meant as much as helping to get Raise the Age passed.

Real Justice didn't stop in Philly. It moved on to another contentious seat that same fall, in Portsmouth, Virginia, where the organization helped reelect Stephanie Morales as DA. Two years earlier, she had successfully charged and convicted a brutal police officer named Stephen Rankin in the murder of a teenage boy named William Chapman II. For years, it was thought that if a DA ever convicted a cop, they could never win reelection, so Real Justice found it essential to back Morales in her reelection bid. And with hard campaigning and on-the-ground support, she did win, bucking the trend.

In the weeks that followed the historic victories of Krasner and Morales, Becky and Zack approached me about joining their small team at Real Justice as a co-founder. I was surprised and humbled by the offer, and after a few weeks of considering it, I joined the team. It was probably the smartest decision I've ever made in my organizing life. For the first time, instead of being the primary leader of an effort, I was just one part of a brilliant team that shared the load. Our small staff was kind, compassionate, and highly skilled. Each of us understood the magnitude of the problems facing us and were more than willing to put in the hard, smart work to do something about them.

With some essential victories under our belt, the team needed to decide which of the 2,400 district attorney seats we would target next. Up and down the state of California, cities from San Diego to Sacramento were scheduled to elect their next district attorneys in the summer and fall of

2018, and we figured that with the right strategies, we could turn the whole state blue. We felt confident about our reach there as well. Becky lived in California full-time and knew it well, as did several of our organizers. Not only had I lived in Southern California off and on for several years, but I had developed a devoted following in the state, through both social media and regular rallies and live events there. I was eager to put it all to good use. Our timing seemed absolutely perfect.

In the 2016 presidential election, Hillary Clinton beat Donald Trump by a whopping 20 percent in San Diego and 25 percent in Sacramento — in other words, complete blowouts. When the team at Real Justice saw that Republican district attorneys were running for reelection in these areas in 2018, we thought it would be a slam dunk for the Democratic candidates. That year was widely being called a blue wave as frustrated Democrats fought back against Trump and conservatives all over the country. If Trump had lost by 20 and 25 percent in those two counties, surely we could run reliable, reform-minded Democrats against his conservative Republican allies and win. So we supported a brilliant, experienced young Black woman named Geneviéve Jones-Wright in her race to be the next district attorney of San Diego. We couldn't have asked for a better, more prepared, more focused candidate; the incumbent wouldn't even show up for many of the local forums and debates. Despite this, we didn't take the race for granted. We helped fuel massive neighborhood canvassing campaigns where we knocked on tens of thousands of doors. We sent thousands of mailers and unique, original, peer-to-peer text messages. We ran radio ads. We sent countless emails. We hosted events. It was our very best work. And we ran on the same message and energy that we had run on in Philadelphia with Larry Krasner — that the justice system needed to be massively overhauled, that brutal police needed to be held accountable, and that the district attorney was the person to make these changes happen.

We repeated this formula in Sacramento. The DA there had literally built a chain-link fence around her office after protests erupted following the shooting death of Stephon Clark, yet another unarmed, nonviolent Black man murdered by police on his own property. Between the blue wave, the energy behind the protests for Stephon Clark, and the fact that Hillary had won the city by 25 percent two years earlier, you couldn't have told me we didn't have Sacramento in the bag. I personally traveled out to California from New York and campaigned all over the state; we played to packed auditoriums everywhere we went. The energy seemed to be there, the strategy was there. We were feeling confident.

Guess what happened? We got our asses handed to us. It wasn't even close. In San Diego, the conservative white Republican candidate won by 32 percent. In Sacramento, we lost to the conservative Republican candidate by 28 percent. The Republican candidates both beat their opponents by a bigger percentage than Hillary had won in those same counties. When we first started our campaigns, I don't think I foresaw a single scenario in which we'd lose. It was hands down one of the worst miscalculations and costly misunderstandings of my life as an organizer. These weren't just campaign losses for us. Our team understands that when we lose, the systems of mass incarceration and police brutality continue unabated in those cities.

I take all of my work so personally that I still think about these losses almost every day. I want to highlight the critical mistakes we made that I think will be particularly instructive for you. First, our team ignored several warning signs about just how hard it was going to be to win in San Diego and Sacramento. Several election experts and pollsters told us that winning against incumbent DAs was always an uphill battle, but I was utterly convinced that they were misreading the tea leaves and didn't understand the moment we were in. I just could not fathom Republican candidates smashing Democratic candidates in places Hillary had won by a landslide. I trusted my hunch, my gut, more than I did the advice of seasoned local experts. Once in a blue moon, going solely by your intuition might work for you, but as a rule, don't ignore the experts. When I look at my biggest failures in business and organizing, they have almost always taken place when I ignored the advice, guidance, and counsel of experienced voices in my life. Sometimes we ask for the advice of the people who know better not because we actually want their advice, but because we are hoping to hear that they believe what we believe. You might not be aware of the fact that you may be going into a conversation seeking validation more than you are seeking advice, but I'm telling you that it happens all the time. And because I want you to stay honest, I advise you to decide in advance what you'll do if those giving you advice strongly advise you against making the decision you *want* to make.

The next two lessons stung the most, in terms of how

they challenged my understanding of how justice could be interpreted in society. First, we learned that the message of radical reform that absolutely crushed it in Philadelphia doesn't necessarily travel everywhere. In Philly, it was widely known that the justice system was deeply corrupt and needed change. Activists and organizers there had been preparing for such a change for decades, and the community responded positively to Larry Krasner's dogged pursuit of justice-oriented lawmaking. Larry already had real credibility in Philadelphia, and the coalition that got behind him was fierce. But not only did our message of change fall flat in San Diego and Sacramento; it was weaponized against us in a way that I just didn't see coming. Put simply, our opponents framed *themselves* as being for safety and security and positioned our candidates as people who were running to give more rights to criminals. And while we fought back on the framing the best we knew how, voters came to believe that the Republican candidates were the ones who cared more about keeping them safe. After all, our candidates, following my advice, hardly said a damn thing about safety, instead focusing on pushing an agenda of sweeping criminal justice reform. It resonated with about 35 percent of the voters and dropped off a cliff after that. That cost us the election. In essence, I learned the wisdom of the old adage "All politics is local." What worked so well for Krasner in Philadelphia could not just be cut and pasted in Southern or Northern California with real success.

Second, we learned something even more upsetting that would inform how we approached every race for district attorney that followed. When we dug into the demographic data of voters in San Diego and Sacramento, we found that, while virtually all Republicans had voted for the Republican incumbent DA, so had a huge chunk of white Democrats who'd voted for Hillary Clinton in 2016. In the end, the voters who showed up for our candidate seemed to be mostly people of color or part of a small faction of white hippies. Virtually everybody else opted to vote in favor of the conservative candidate. My calculation that a vote for Hillary would subsequently translate to a vote for a Democratic candidate running for district attorney was off in one key way: people vote for their own interests. Period. Millions of white voters in California had seen voting for Hillary—or voting against Donald Trump—in 2016 as a vote for their own interests. That's what gets people to the polls. And when we asked voters in San Diego and Sacramento to basically vote against mass incarceration, 65 percent of them saw what we were proposing as a vote against their own interests. They simply did not see ending mass incarceration and police brutality as good enough reasons to change the status quo. The lesson in that is this: when crafting a campaign for a candidate or cause, you must appeal to the unique self-interests of enough voters to win the election. Everything we campaigned on was noble and good, but we still got our asses whupped. That wasn't the point of running those races. The point was to win. And if we needed to significantly change our messaging or marketing in order to win, we damn sure should've done it.

I am an abolitionist at heart. I want to see the systems and structures of mass incarceration completely torn down.

The laws and the selective application of the laws are all about power and control, not justice, fairness, or safety. I'd like to reimagine something truly just and honorable and restorative in its place. But if that message loses elections, if it causes horrible people to remain in power, if it impedes real, measurable, tangible change from taking place, then I have to ask myself whether my ideological purity is helping or harming the cause. And that's not to say that I don't think there's room for purists; I actually welcome them. They move the needle of the conversation in essential ways. Without them, our hopes and expectations would be far too low. But sometimes, to win key battles, you have to campaign on more than revolution. You have to accept that not everybody sees the world the way you see it, and that in order to get some of what you want done, you may have to pitch it differently.

At the end of the day, we spent the most money we had ever raised for those races in California, and yet we got crushed. And now San Diego and Sacramento have conservatives running their justice systems at a time when progressives should be in those cities making meaningful reforms. Our miscalculations, our lack of understanding of who and what message could win in those cities, our underestimation of our opponents, and our flat-out ignorance of the willingness of moderate white Democrats to swing conservative when it came to the justice system all worked against us. The losses weren't our fault alone, but we damn sure weren't organized to win. And that always has to be the calculus. What will it take to get 51 percent of the vote? Sometimes winning might not be the main goal of your organiz-ing—sometimes it might be awareness or solidarity or team building—but if your goal is to win an election or to get legislation passed, you have to organize to win. And that's a whole different equation than organizing for awareness.

Our team was devastated by the losses in San Diego and Sacramento. We also lost to the more conservative can-didate in Alameda County, which includes Oakland and Berkeley. All of that flew in the face of California being a liberal stronghold. Up and down the state, voters chose the most conservative candidate to run their local justice sys-tem. But instead of simply lamenting the losses and sink-ing into a deep depression, which I damn sure wanted to do, we refused to put our heads in the sand. We immediately began a brutal process of self-reflection in order to under-stand what went wrong and how we could avoid making those same mistakes again. We squeezed as many lessons out of the losses as we could and used them to inform all of the other candidates we were supporting across the coun-try. With our newly improved strategy, we soon won a huge race in San Antonio, Texas, where we ousted a horrible dis-trict attorney and replaced him with a compassionate man named Joe Gonzales.

And I'm pleased to say that we followed Gonzales's elec-tion with two of our most groundbreaking and historic vic-tories. In St. Louis, a young Black man named Wesley Bell decided to challenge Bob McCulloch, who had served as DA of St. Louis County since Bell was a child. After graduat-ing from law school, Bell served as a public defender in St. Louis before eventually being elected to the Ferguson City

Council in 2015, with the backing of the activist and organizing community there. The fact that Wesley was challenging Bob McCulloch was historic in and of itself. McCulloch had been in office for generations and was the king of mass incarceration for St. Louis County, part of a system that threw the book at Black people for each and every infraction while protecting cops at all costs.

Initially, Wesley Bell was seen as a long-shot candidate at best. The political machine may have backed one man for generations, but it was the strategy of local organizers and activists, with all of the lessons they had learned on the ground over the previous four years, that fueled Bell's campaign. Our team at Real Justice was quick to inform him of the lessons we'd learned from our painful losses in California and began crafting a revised message for his marketing materials and talking points. Instead of just addressing injustice and mass incarceration, we encouraged Wesley to adopt a platform of public safety. We even encouraged him to talk about police brutality and mass incarceration through that lens, emphasizing how those social problems actually made St. Louis less safe and pulled essential resources away from the issues that mattered most to voters. We were able to give this sage, effective advice only because our team was in a constant state of analysis and planning, allowing us to optimize the message in real time. All of this hard work paid off, and Wesley Bell defeated Bob McCulloch by 14 percent, becoming the first African American district attorney in the history of St. Louis County. Inspired by other progressive DAs around the country, he hit the ground running by firing several career prosecutors who refused to adopt his agenda of change. He has since formed an integrity review unit to oversee questionable prosecutions and has started reforming the policies on cash bail, sentencing, parole, and probation, as well as rehabilitation and diversion programs.

In Boston, my dear friend Rachael Rollins stepped up to run for DA of Boston and Suffolk County, Massachusetts. Rachael is tough as nails. Raised by a mother who was an immigrant from the West Indies, and an Irish American father who was a military veteran and corrections officer, Rachael played Division I lacrosse in college and went on to become a federal prosecutor and the chief legal counsel for the Massachusetts Port Authority. When she decided to run, the odds seemed insurmountable—since its founding in 1630, the city of Boston had never had a woman or an African American serve as DA. In fact, in the entire history of Massachusetts, not a single woman of color had ever been elected district attorney. Early polls predicted she'd lose by double digits. Still, she was undeterred. Running on a message of change, reform, and safety, Rachael Rollins ended up winning 80 percent of the vote and started changing the system there right out of the gate.

Our new focus on public safety messaging with our candidates was a winning one. Of course, each candidate had to contextualize that message for their own city, but making the pivot made a huge difference for each of them. With those lessons learned, we went on to win races for DA in Arlington, Virginia, with Parisa Dehghani-Tafti, who was an attorney for the Innocence Project, and in Fairfax, Virginia, with Steve Descano, a former prosecutor from the Obama administration. We also helped to elect Jody Owens, a civil rights attorney for the Southern Poverty Law Center, as the new DA of Jackson, Mississippi. But no victory meant more to me than that of my friend and brother Chesa Boudin, who became the new district attorney of San Francisco. On the very first episode of my podcast *The Breakdown*, I chose to tell Chesa's story. The nation has never had a DA like him.

Chesa's parents, David Gilbert and Kathy Boudin, members of the leftist group the Weather Underground, were convicted of the 1981 murders of two police officers and a guard for an armored truck. While his parents didn't actually shoot anyone—they were driving the getaway truck—under the law, they were charged as harshly as someone who had committed felony murder. Chesa was just fourteen months old and grew up regularly visiting both of his parents in the harshest prison conditions imaginable. His mother spent twenty-two years in prison, but his father is not eligible for parole until 2056. We call that the slow death penalty. Chesa, a brilliant Rhodes scholar, was raised to be a compassionate lover of civil and human rights, and he went on to become one of the most respected public defenders in San Francisco. The notion that he could ever run the local justice system there seemed preposterous to many. The governor, the lieutenant governor, and both U.S. senators endorsed his opponent, as did the *San Francisco Chronicle*, the mayors of Oakland and San Francisco, and a number of U.S. congresspeople. Local police unions, as well as police unions from Los Angeles, New York, Seattle, and Portland, each contributed thousands of dollars to his opponent. With the odds stacked against him, Chesa shocked everybody by winning. He out-organized his opponents in every way, and his message of deep reforms, real accountability, and public safety resonated with the majority of voters. His win and the deep systemic changes he is already making represent one of the sweetest victories of my life as an organizer. Our team at Real Justice has lost eleven painful races for DA, and I don't think we could've helped Chesa Boudin win in San Francisco without the lessons we learned from each race preceding his.

When you organize for change, particularly if you are charting new territory and fighting against the status quo, you are sometimes going to make big bets and take risky gambles—and lose. Even with all of your hard work and preparation and organization, you're not always going to win—not in electoral politics, not in courtrooms or boardrooms, and certainly not on legislative floors. Wins are hard to come by in all of those places. When you have them, celebrate, and when you don't, try your best to learn whatever you can from the losses and keep moving forward. Above all, be honest about your mistakes. That's easier than it sounds. For me, it means having trusted, sincere people in my life who will always tell me the good, bad, and ugly of who I am and what I'm doing. Self-reflection is great, but sometimes you need friends and confidants to give you earnest feedback as well. And when you approach organizing with that sort of radical honesty and self-reflection, I guarantee you're going to find yourself a stronger, better, and more informed person in this fight for change.

11

# Burnout and Revolutionary Self-Care

ALL AT THE SAME TIME, this world can be so beautiful, so miraculous, and yet can also be so immeasurably ugly.

When I first wrote this chapter, I was on an early-morning flight from Dallas, Texas, back home to New York to be with my family. As I glanced out of the window next to me, the view of the sunrise above the earth took my breath away. The colors were so spectacular — orange, pink, red, and blue — that it seemed like an artist had put it all out there just for me to see. As I moved my gaze from the marvelous sunrise back to my computer, I was quickly brought down to earth. Donald Trump had just tweeted that a civil war might break out if he was impeached. A family had just emailed me to say that their son had been shot and killed by police that weekend. Four other families had sent me some version of the same message about their own sons losing their lives to police violence over the past week. I had just left Dallas after speaking for the family of Botham Jean on what would have been his twenty-eighth birthday, had he not been shot and killed by a police officer in his own home. Suddenly, a heavy burden overcame me. To be alive in this age is to be hyper-informed of all that is good *and* all that is horrible in the world. And the beauty of the sunrise juxtaposed against all the violence and trauma happening under its warm glow nearly brought me to tears.

My greatest superpower is that I am a deeply sensitive person. I take the pain of other people, complete strangers, so personally that over the course of each day I can pinball between fury, grief, and despair. I absorb their pain, make it my own, then use it to fuel the advocacy and work I do on their behalf. Speaking, writing, and organizing with such urgency has allowed me to break through the noise of our world. But absorbing so much pain, day in and day out, for years on end, is also my greatest weakness. It makes it difficult, nearly impossible, for me to say no. Sometimes when people come to me asking for help, it took them everything they had to even figure out how to contact me. They will text and call my friends and family. They will arrive hours before a speaking engagement and wait at the entrance they think I'll be using. They'll defy security and come backstage moments before an event begins. They'll wait until an event is over and the entire crowd has left, in the hope that they will get just a few minutes alone with me to plead their case. They desperately need help and have been told, correctly, that I am likely to say yes. Maybe it's because I know what it feels like to need help and not get it, but whatever the case, I struggle to say no when someone who is desperate and hurting asks for my help. And before I know it, I have said yes to more people and obligations than any one person could ever effectively manage.

What I have had to accept, as painful as it is for me and for others, is that saying yes to everybody is, in fact, saying no to the cause I care about the most. For any of us to be effective citizens, particularly if our goal is serious systemic change, we have to practice compassionately telling people no and pointing them to other people and resources that can better serve them. This is never easy for me, and in the past, out of a desire to be kind or sometimes just in an attempt not to disappoint people, I said yes to so many requests and demands that I could never possibly honor them all—which ultimately just caused those people to be even more frustrated and disappointed than if I had respectfully stepped aside from the start. I have to regularly remind myself that I am a finite being, with limited time and resources, and that in order to best serve the causes I have dedicated my life to, I must remain disciplined in my daily focus.

If you, too, are someone who takes the pain of the world personally, what is a regular day for others can be overwhelming for you. The cycles of violence and despair that we are in, with so much trauma and so little change or justice, can sometimes be too much for the average person to handle. I do not believe our brains or hearts were built to accept so much ugliness. One of the central reasons I am an organizer and an activist is because fighting for change is cathartic for me. Knowing that I have tried and given my best each day gives me peace of mind in the midst of a very

chaotic world. Some days I am disappointed that my best effort was not good enough to make the impact I hoped and
fought for, but I have learned the hard lesson that many outcomes are simply beyond my grasp. Other days, fully ex-
hausted and having given it my all, I go to bed knowing that
I wasn't able to do even half of what I'd hoped I could accomplish. On all those days I have to repeat this mantra in
my head: *It was my best. It was my best. It was my best.* Sometimes that helps.

This is a good place to introduce you to Audre Lorde.
Born to Caribbean immigrant parents in New York City in
1934, Lorde was a brilliant thinker, writer, poet, womanist,
and activist. She often wrote and spoke about what it meant
to live outside of the bubble of the norms and expectations
of society. And even though she passed away years ago, her
words are frequently invoked today to serve as a balm for
our souls. Perhaps nothing is more apt here than when she
said, "Caring for myself is not self-indulgence, it is self-pres-
ervation, and that is an act of political warfare."

Intuitively, I know that Audre Lorde was right. Of course
she was. Caring for ourselves, for our mental and emotional health, for our physical well-being—that is not self-
indulgent or extra. It is essential! It is not just important but
righteous. However, my mind rarely processes it as such. I
have programmed it over the years to fully believe that the
only thing of value is serving others. I am embarrassed to
say it, but I think that at the root of that type of thinking is
the painful thought that maybe I am not worth taking care
of—that I am only as useful and valuable as my ability to
help someone else. It stings me to even see those words on

this page, but functionally, I have operated under that reality for most of my life, until the past year or so. I say that because I want to admit to you that I am not some wise old sage on the topic of self-care. Maybe like you, I am new to it. And still have to trick my mind into accepting that I am worthy of it. But I need it, and I deserve it, and so do you.

The work of activism can be deeply traumatic. Activists are often called to be present to people and communities in moments of great pain, disaster, and unspeakable despair. At the height of our efforts in 2014, on some days I would study a video of a police shooting hundreds of times, slowing it down to view it frame by frame, zooming in and out, looking for clues, all so that I could better communicate to the world in the most concrete terms just how unjust such shootings truly are. It was during that process that I realized the Ferguson Police Department and the neighboring St. Louis County Police Department had told a crucial lie from the start about the shooting death of unarmed teenager Michael Brown. Police repeatedly claimed on the record that the shooting had been unavoidable and had taken place within thirty-five feet of the SUV of Officer Darren Wilson. In the absence of a body camera video, it was important for police to paint a narrative of a close-up encounter. But as I pored over every photo and video and interview, I soon realized that it was a total fabrication. Michael Brown ran for his life that day — not thirty-five feet, or seventy-five feet, or 105 feet . . . Michael Brown ran more than fifty yards, a total distance of 153 feet — before he was repeatedly shot and killed by Darren Wilson. I know because I paid to have it professionally measured. For nearly two hundred days I demanded that the police departments address this discrepancy in their story, but they refused, instead sticking to their story of a close-up encounter. Only after the prosecutor announced that no charges were going to be filed and all of the records were released did they admit in their document dump that my understanding of the situation was correct. But by that time, as police and prosecutors so often do, they had already cleared themselves of any wrongdoing, leaving the family and community at large shattered, angry, and without any measure of resolution. Police murders are, of course, destructive to the mental health of the community, but the denial of justice causes its own form of anguish.

I cannot underscore enough the importance of trying to keep mentally strong when you come across these points of trauma and to acknowledge their weight. As a student of history, I don't know why I was surprised by the vitriol and bigotry that came my way as soon as I started publicly fighting against police brutality, but it did surprise me. In the fall of 2014, when I would advocate for Michael Brown or Eric Garner on social media, I would regularly be called a nigger and be threatened with death. I had not been called a nigger in nearly twenty years and had not expected it to happen again for the rest of my life. I did not yet have any knowledge of Leopold von Ranke and how human beings aren't necessarily getting better and better over time. Just days after Michael Brown was murdered in Ferguson, somebody found a picture of my kids, Photoshopped them being shot and killed, and posted it on social media. I was an early adopter of social media and had actually been on Twitter since early 2007, when it consisted of just a few hundred thousand nerds. By the time Michael Brown was murdered, seven years later, I had already written more than 100,000 tweets and had never, not one single time, been the target of a racial slur, or anything hateful, for that matter. I damn sure never had someone threaten to kill me or my family. As my public role increased, the venom directed my way instantly did as well.

It takes a great deal of discipline to read and see so much hate about yourself all over the internet and not internalize it. I soon realized that, to protect my heart and mind from all of the ugliness, from the insulting memes and names, from the threats and lies, I had flipped a switch that allowed me to stop caring about what people said about me. It was not a healthy switch, but it was an instinctual, protective response. When I flipped that switch, however, I not only stopped caring about what trolls and haters had to say about me; I unwittingly stopped caring about what *anybody* had to say—including friends, family, and colleagues. My brain began processing thoughtful criticism from loved ones the same way it processed destructive remarks from strangers. They all meant nothing to me.

As my wife and kids began hinting at my emotional distance, saying that I was physically present but an emotional ghost, I could not explain it. I knew that I loved them. I cared for them. They were special to me. But the emotional toll of my work had stolen my light. To protect myself from enemies, I had walled off my heart from everyone. This is a new revelation for me that I am still unraveling. It took devastating heart-to-heart conversations with my wife and kids for me to fully understand that I had lost years of quality time with them in the name of fighting for justice and making change. I told myself that I was doing all this for them, so that the world they lived in would be a much better place, and on many levels that was true. But it hindered me from being fully alive, fully present, fully connected to them. Most of my heroes either were assassinated, drove their families into the ground in the name of doing good, or both. I see now that good intentions can lead any of us to those ends, and I struggle with that knowledge.

Clearly, I am far from an expert in self-care. One of my dear friends called me a wounded healer. I am more of a survivor than anything else, but I have learned a few practices that have helped me get this far in nearly one piece, and I'd like to share them with you. Again, these are the practices that work for me. Part of your journey will be finding the habits and disciplines that work for you. If anything I suggest seems like a square peg for a round hole in your life, don't sweat it, but I hope something here resonates with you.

Therapy is a critical aspect of how I try to keep moving forward in a healthy, balanced way. My wife and I have been to marriage counseling on multiple occasions, and everybody in our house has seen a therapist. Counselors and therapists are simply expert guides, and we all need them. At first, I was the stereotypical man, in that I was super slow to admit that I needed help and definitely waited too long to go, but therapy has been transformative for me. We need to be attentive to our minds and our emotions, just like every other aspect of our health, but often we pretend otherwise.

Over the course of my life, I have never been suicidal, but

I have, on three or four occasions, allowed myself to sink into such a deep pit of despair that I struggled to find my way out of it. After my second spinal surgery when I was assaulted in high school, I was in that place, with PTSD, and I felt like giving up. I found myself there yet again four years later, after yet another emergency spinal surgery stemming from the same injuries forced me to step down as student government president at Morehouse and take a leave of absence. I was devastated. In 2011, when I resigned as pastor of the church I'd started and moved our family from Atlanta to Southern California, I was in a fog for months. My only dream during the previous decade was to be a pastor. I had placed so much of my identity and self-worth in that dream that I struggled to know who I was without that role. In the worst moments, particularly after some of my biggest failures as a leader and organizer, I have found myself no longer being fond of this world and all of its ugliness. Thankfully, skilled guides and mentors have helped me navigate those valleys until I found my way out. They have always reminded me that my friends and family love me far more than my worst enemies hate me. And that the sting of the worst attacks against me, even if I am trending across social media for a lie, will eventually fade away.

I am grateful for a small number of friends with whom I can share every single thing going on in my world. The pressure of maintaining every burden of my heart and mind all by myself is simply too much for me to handle. If the world has beaten me down and I begin to grow weary, I try my best to tell someone who I know loves me. It doesn't make the problem go away, of course, but it eases the heaviness of it if I can share it with my crew. Fighting for change can sometimes be thankless, lonely work. And social media is a piss-poor substitute for offline friendships in the lowest moments. I have learned to value my trusted friends more than all of the social media followers in the world. You need to keep the same thing in mind. Social media can often be a toxic place. You are not the sum total of the worst tweets ever said about you. I have had to learn not to allow strangers or bots or paid trolls, who don't even know me and have never met me or my loved ones, to define me. The same applies to you. You're better than that.

My phone is the source of a lot of anxiety in my life. Now, I love that damn phone for the music and movies I enjoy from it and the pictures I take and peruse, but it's also my conduit to all of the horrible news of the world. From the social media apps to the news apps to the constant barrage of text messages and phone calls I get, bad news could dominate every waking hour of my day if I let it. So I have to set healthy boundaries with my phone. We are fully addicted to these devices. Have you ever left the house without it and felt a sudden panic come over you? Or have you ever felt it vibrate or heard it ring, only to realize it was all in your head? We've got problems! One recent medical study suggested that humans are looking down at their phones so much that our bones are changing shape in our necks as a result. It's literally changing our biology! We must be more conscious of this, both for social relations and for our mental health.

As a general rule, I don't bring my phone to the dinner table. We try to have dinner together as a family every night, and the last thing we need is all of us looking at our phones, so we leave them far away from the table. It allows us to simply enjoy the food and one another's company. I do the same thing on dates with my wife. Unless we are checking on the kids, our dates are phone-free events. That's easier said than done, but having those few hours of quality time sometimes makes all the difference in our marriage. I'm sure the same is true for you, whether you are married or not. Try to break the addictive habit of being on your phone, and just *be* in the world. Find phone-free spaces and places in your life so that you can be fully present in that moment. My wife and I often go to a phone-free movie theater, and I love it so much. The usher will literally kick you out of the theater without a refund if you check your phone. It's our favorite place! During those few hours, I forget about the whole world and just enjoy that movie. It feels like we're back in the nineties. If you can't find places where phones are banned, make your own phone-free rules, whether that means putting your phone in another room while you're with your family or friends or not checking it after a certain time.

To be effective in our relationships and in our activism, we need focus and clarity. Our phones are distraction machines. When I am leading meetings or on panels, or when I am a keynote speaker somewhere, I put my phone on airplane mode, pack it away, and make sure that I don't check it. I look people in the eye. I listen intently and reply thoughtfully. Technology has caused us to lose some basic social graces, and I think we forget how rude we look when we are checking our phones during essential meetings and gatherings. I try hard to be fully present, physically and emotionally, when I am in meetings. If I don't think that's possible, because an emergency or deadline is just too pressing, I try to reschedule, particularly if the meeting's success hinges on my presence. Whatever the case, if I go to a meeting, I am fully there. We should all try to be more present, even if it means taking a hard look at our phone habits.

And then there are the little things that I do to reset and recharge. It may sound simple, but both music and comedy have always helped me in this way. I'm a huge a fan of hip-hop and stand-up. By no means am I saying that a good Nipsey Hussle track is the cure for clinical depression, but his music, and music from artists ranging from Donny Hathaway and Johnny Cash to Jidenna and Bob Marley, routinely lifts my spirit and self-esteem. Music therapy is a real thing. And laughter is that way, too. I could listen to the best stand-up comedians all day long. I'm a lifelong Richard Pryor fan and regularly listen to his old comedy records when I'm down. Onstage, Richard often talked about his journey in the most hilarious ways. All I am saying is that when you are down, try changing the soundtrack of your life. It helps me.

And as shallow as this sounds, a fresh haircut always gives me a major boost. I don't care if a single soul sees it—that doesn't matter so much to me—but I love the way a sharp haircut makes me feel. I try to get one at least every two weeks or so. I feel goofy saying this, but for those first few days afterward, I feel invincible.

I am also a firm believer in something I call energetic rhythms. In every twenty-four-hour cycle, each of us has a few hours when we are at our energetic best. For me, that is probably from 9 a.m. to 12 noon. I wake up much earlier than that and work much later, but during those three power hours, I am at my most alert. My mind is clear and I am able to focus, so I try and do my best, most important work during those hours. Your best few hours may be at a different time of day, but regardless of the timing, you don't want to waste them chasing random emails. If you can, give yourself a few scheduled points in the day when you check your email, and spend the rest of the time doing what is central to your life and cause. One of the reasons so many causes struggle is that the only time people can afford to give them is tacked on after a hard day's work. For a while that may be the case, but make it your goal to figure out how to give the cause you care about most some of your best time.

My work ethic has deep roots. I grew up in a house with a mother who worked at least forty or fifty hours a week for nearly forty-five years, making lightbulbs in a brutally hot factory in rural Kentucky. I don't remember her ever being sick a day in my life. She'd leave the house at the crack of dawn, fresh and clean, and come back home every day drenched in sweat. She instilled that work ethic in me from a young age. I work so hard that I usually have to be stopped and pulled away from my work. That being said, I still take days off. We take vacations together as a family when we can. I take days off from social media, sometimes letting trusted colleagues take over the account when I need to be away. I take days off from my work responsibilities. And when I do so, I do it knowing that it's the only way I can sustain the pace and depth of my activism and organizing. What does a day off look like for you? I hope they aren't all used for errands and grocery shopping, because you must schedule time to really check out.

None of us can be *on* 24/7. Keep that in mind. Except in rare emergencies, I don't take phone calls after 7 p.m. I rarely respond to emails after 7 p.m., either. If I'm in town, I reserve 7 to 10 p.m. nightly to be with my family. We eat dinner, we talk openly about our day, we play board games. We might curl up and watch a family TV show together. I might watch an NBA game with my son. But by the time 7 p.m. comes, I typically have already worked twelve to fourteen hours that day. That's enough. I normally still have an endless amount of work that I could continue plowing through, but it's more important, for my own well-being and for the health of my family, to find a reasonable time to transition out of it. I took me a while to learn that we teach people how to treat us. If we answer the phone at 10 p.m., people will keep calling at 10 p.m. If we answer emails at 2 a.m., people will expect you to keep doing so. But when we teach people that we are most likely to respond and engage with them during some semblance of business hours, they'll get the picture that we have boundaries.

Your path to self-care will likely look very different from mine, but I just want you to understand that you *need* to be on this path. It's not an admission of defeat. It's an admission that you are human. And self-care is like hydration: if you are feeling thirsty, you're already behind. Make self-care a part of your life when you are well, and the disciplines, habits, and boundaries that you establish will be there when you need them the most. You bought this book to learn how to make change. What I know is that the process of making change requires you to be as healthy and whole as humanly possible, and that nobody is going to care about your wellness more than you.

## 12

# It's on Us

WHEN I ARRIVED at Morehouse in 1997, only a few of the admissions officers and administrators had any idea what I had gone through in high school. It was in me, but when I got to Morehouse, I didn't necessarily want what I had overcome to define me. I did not want to be known as the student who had survived a brutal assault by a bunch of racists. Two years later, a teenage boy from South Central Los Angeles named Lee Merritt arrived at Morehouse with his own survival story that he also held close to his chest. Not only had Lee grown up in South Central at the height of gang violence and the war on drugs, but he was raised by Crips from birth. His father, known as Murder Roc, and his uncles Bone, JB, and Bud were all notorious members of the Rollin 60's Neighborhood Crips. His father, uncles, and older brothers were all caught up in a vicious cycle of violence and incarceration. When Lee dropped out of high school and moved in with his grandmother, his entire life was on thin ice, and many expected that he would soon take the route of those who'd come before him. He narrowly escaped that destiny, and he ended up alongside me in the same close-knit Atlanta community of brothers that ultimately changed both of our lives.

More than twenty years later, Lee is my best friend and closest partner in the fight for justice and community empowerment. He is now one of the most important and effective civil rights attorneys in the world. Last year, when Lee and I sat down to think back on all of the projects we had worked on together, and all of the families we had helped over the years, we could hardly believe it. Day in and day out, we did the work without really tracking or measuring the impact, but when we finally sat down to evaluate it, we were humbled by all that we had been able to accomplish together. In some ways, we chose to do this work, but in other ways, it chose us.

In case after case of police violence, of bigotry and white supremacy, we kept thinking that somebody else was going to step up and intervene and advocate for the victims, but they never did. Sometimes we would hold off on providing support in the hope that somebody else would step up. When they didn't, Lee would say three simple words that we now repeat to each other almost every day: "It's on us."

That phrase has become a mantra for us. The government, corporations, and other megaorganizations absolutely have a real responsibility to do right by people, and I am all for holding them accountable. But I've come to understand that the change we want to see in the world is not going to happen until we stand up, organize, and make it happen ourselves. The American government was not created for equality or harmony or fairness or any other warm and fuzzy purpose. It was created for white power. Even more specifically, it was created to protect and advance privileged white men. Anything it does beyond that narrow scope has to be forced.

Corporations, with rare exceptions, are no different. They exist primarily to produce profits and build wealth for their shareholders. They regularly bulldoze over people and principles in the pursuit of profits. That's their mission. To get them to operate outside of that standard practice normally takes a humiliating scandal, a highly organized movement, or a mix of both.

This may be hard to hear, but even most of the nation's leading charities don't exist for revolution or transformation. Very few of them disrupt the status quo. They are rarely designed to get to the root of problems and build solutions from the ground up. Instead, America's charitable machine too often treats symptoms in perpetuity while allowing root causes to remain entrenched for generations. A huge percentage of their boards and advisers come from either corporate America or the government. I applaud and donate to organizations that provide hungry people with meals, but I'd rather figure out how the richest country in the history of the world can close the disparities that produce so much hunger and poverty in the first place. But that's the rub. In an age when the gap between the superrich and everybody else is wider than it's ever been, the superrich have no interest in changing the fundamental calculus that allowed them to gain such wealth in the first place. They have no problem with charities, as long as those charities don't interrupt their profits or power in any significant ways.

The world does not lack government agencies, corporations, or organizations — they operate in abundance in perfect parallel to the greatest problems we face. What the world lacks is highly energized, deeply organized, sufficiently strategized people and movements that interrupt the way things are and the way things will continue to be. The future we dream of for ourselves and for the generations to come will not simply happen naturally. We have to force that future into existence. We have to imagine and build it ourselves.

I have to be clear about what I mean when I say "It's on us." I mean it's on *you,* my friend. If you picked up this book, it's because you have a heart to make change. You know this world is not living up to its full potential. You are fully aware that the systems and structures of oppression and inequity aren't inevitable. They can be torn down. We've torn them down before. And we can tear them down again. We must. You must. And you can.

I wrote this book to give you insight into my life and journey, but more than that, I wrote it because the world needs you to step up in ways you've never stepped up before. What Lee and I found is true: if you have a heart to address a crisis in the world, waiting for another rescue team to show up is more than likely going to be futile. Instead, I am asking you to lean into that feeling. It's a sign. It's a clue. It's a hint that it's *your* time to make change. Instead of ignoring the quiet voice inside you that is beckoning you to action, acknowledge it, honor it, and become an agent of change.

Right here, right now, you have every single thing you need to take the first step. You don't need a certain type of college education. You don't need special permission. You don't have to be a person of influence with all types of connections. You don't need a big following on social media. You don't have to be wealthy or a person of means. You don't have to have a spotless past. You don't have to know the beginning, middle, and end of your journey. You just have to have a heart for change and a willingness to take the first steps toward making it.

Do not talk yourself out of making change. Do not convince yourself that you are unimportant or that your contributions will be insignificant or inconsequential. Do not allow yourself to believe the lie that the way things are now is just the way things are always going to be. Do not think for a single, solitary moment that you aren't cut out for this. Quite the opposite! I believe with all of my heart that you were made for this exact moment in time. You were born and raised and now live in this era for a reason. This time —this dip—that we now find ourselves in needs you. And when you look the other way, you are denying the essence of your best self.

In the summer of 2014, it was a simple Facebook message from a friend who sent me the horrible video of the lynching of Eric Garner that changed the entire trajectory of my life. At that very moment, I knew I had to figure out how I could do something, anything, that would make a difference in that case, and since then, I have dedicated the rest of my days to fighting for racial and social justice. I have tried to document in this book many of my successes and struggles in that endeavor. I never expected, in the middle of writing this book, that I'd so clearly see the action steps for organizing put into action. But that's exactly what happened in the case of Rodney Reed.

I have long been against the death penalty. But that's not what drew me to the case of Rodney Reed, a Texas man who was sentenced to death in 1998 and was still on death row. Instead, it was a simple question from my wife on the morning of November 1, 2019, that inspired me to use every single lesson I have learned as an activist to help save his life. On that day, as we were getting dressed and ready to take the kids to school, Rai held up her iPhone to show me a news story about Rodney Reed's impending execution date —November 20, just nineteen days away. She asked me if I had heard of his case.

I had. My first clear memory of hearing about Rodney's case was in 2015, when he was, once again, just days away from being executed. Thanks to the tireless efforts of my friends at the Innocence Project, he was granted an appeal. In the years since, I had heard updates about his case here and there and saw that several TV documentaries had been made about it, but I never thought about getting involved.

Almost every developed nation in the world has abolished the death penalty. It's barbaric. And beyond that, in the United States, it is disproportionately reserved for poor men of color. As a rule, rich people are rarely executed, no matter how heinous the crime they commit. They can afford the best attorneys to ensure that never happens. And nobody is more likely to be executed than a Black man convicted of killing a white woman.

Such was the story of Rodney Reed, who was found guilty of the murder of a young white woman named Stacey Stites by an all-white jury. Hours after my wife mentioned Rodney's case, I began studying it, gathering source documents, court transcripts, police reports, legal briefs, as well as audio and video interviews with witnesses and experts. If there's one thing I've learned, it's that you can't effectively fight to solve a problem if you don't truly understand the complexity and nuances of it.

Earlier that same afternoon, I called Lee Merritt to see what he knew about it. Two weeks prior, Lee had appeared on the *Dr. Phil* show with the family of Botham Jean soon after Amber Guyger, the officer who shot him in his own home, had been convicted for his murder. Lee told me that Dr. Phil had just spent over a month researching Rodney Reed's case and had met with nearly two dozen experts and interviewed Rodney in prison. He then hosted two full episodes of his show where he stated his belief that the State of Texas was about to execute an innocent man.

I watched both episodes of the *Dr. Phil* show that same day and was also convinced. Dr. Phil brought in four respected forensic scientists, three of whom testified in affidavits that they believed it was scientifically impossible for Rodney Reed to have committed the murder. Likewise, a number of experienced law enforcement officers and detectives who had studied the evidence at great length determined that Rodney Reed was not guilty. The prosecution's entire case against Rodney hinged on him being a stranger who somehow carjacked Stacey Stites on an old country road while she was on her way to work at 3 a.m. at a local grocery store.

But Dr. Phil brought forth witnesses, including one of the victim's co-workers, who testified that Stacey had told her she had been in a relationship with Rodney, which would explain why his DNA was found on her. On the show, witnesses said they believed that her fiancé, a local police officer named Jimmy Fennell, was the one who had murdered her. It wasn't a difficult leap. While on duty one day after Stites was murdered, Fennell kidnapped and sexually assaulted a woman, a crime he was convicted of and spent ten years in prison for. Dr. Phil presented witnesses who revealed that Fennell had lied about his alibi for the time when Stites was murdered, that DNA of some fellow law enforcement officers has been found on fresh beer cans next to her body, and that Fennell had been out drinking hours before her murder.

From the day Rodney was convicted, people have doubted the fairness of his trial and the integrity of the evidence, including the fact that the prosecution has refused to test the murder weapon for DNA. As I was doing my deep dive on the case, I also saw that one of my heroes, Sister Helen Prejean, was tweeting in Rodney's defense. Her autobiography, *Dead Man Walking*, inspired the movie that is based on her ministry to men on death row. I had befriended Helen the previous year and DMed her to let her know I wanted to help. She responded, delighted that I wanted to use my platform to advocate for Rodney, and connected me to Rodney's younger brother, Rodrick. Rodrick texted me, and within minutes we were speaking. He told me he was happy to hear that someone with a big audience was willing to help him with the case.

"We have been fighting for Rodney for over twenty years," he told me.

When he said that, the size of the injustice hit me hard. For twenty years—a generation—this family had a loved one behind bars, and had been fighting not just for his release, but for his life.

On that call, I pledged to Rodrick that I would fight relentlessly to stop the execution. Rodrick then gave me explicit permission to do whatever was necessary, to say whatever I needed to say, if I thought it could make a difference. That gave me the peace of mind to move forward full steam ahead.

With Rodrick's approval to advocate on his brother's behalf, I dropped everything else in my life to focus entirely on the case. We could not save Eric or Michael or Tamir or the hundreds of people that I had advocated for posthumously, but here we had the chance to prevent an unjust death.

I got on the phone with the brilliant team at the Action PAC, including my dear friends Becky Bond and Zack Malitz from Real Justice, as well as nearly twenty additional staff members, who are among the most skilled, compassionate, and nimble organizers I've ever encountered. Lyssandra, Jin, Zöe, Dan, Kenneth, Adem, Sean, Damien, Rob, and others all immediately grasped the urgency of the matter and started setting the wheels in motion for us to launch a petition for Rodney Reed and to use the petition to mobilize volunteers in supersmart, effective ways.

Once everyone unanimously agreed to do this work, I started making calls to my attorney friends in Texas to learn what we were up against. I wanted to hear from people who intimately knew the complicated nature of Texas politics, to understand the challenges ahead. One such call was to Bryce Benjet, Rodney's lead attorney from the Innocence Project. He explained that three main parties had the power to stop the execution — the governor, the Board of Pardons and Paroles, and the local district attorney — and that our influence would best be used to do two primary things: first, to make Rodney's case go super-viral, and second, to do our best to lobby those three parties.

It only took twenty-four hours, which typically would've been lightning speed, but in this instance it meant one more day had passed, and Rodney Reed now had just seventeen days left before his execution.

I still had not mentioned publicly that I was going to be working on Rodney's case. I've learned over the years that you get only one opportunity to launch a campaign, especially one with stakes this high. We knew that we had to hit all the right notes, come out strong, and be ready to respond to everyone who would want to help. If you don't nail your first impression, all is not lost, but it can make the job so much harder. Throughout the night, our team built our own petition website, wrote and edited compelling copy for it, and bought the domain FreeRodneyReed .com. We barely slept as we prepared to launch the campaign that morning.

Before we announced it publicly, we took our website live and ran tests on every form and every link to make sure they all worked well. I then asked Rodney's family to send me as many photos of their loved one as possible, a critical step that I now regularly implement in our messaging. Police, prosecutors, and mainstream media go out of their way to show mug shots and demeaning, dehumanizing photos of Black folk who've been arrested. It's part of how they set their tone and agenda. To counterbalance that, I've learned that it's important to introduce the public to a person through photos that display their humanity and warmth in a way that a mug shot never could.

I settled on a photo of Rodney behind prison glass, holding up photos of his children and grandchildren, as the first image I would use to introduce him to the world. I changed all of the links on all of my social media page bios to FreeRodneyReed.com. Then I went to Instagram, which is where I typically first announce every new project and case I am working on, as I find the community there to be warmer and more humane.

When we were ready to launch, I wrote the following caption:

EMERGENCY! I mean that literally. Do you hear me? This is an emergency. In just 16 days the State of Texas is scheduled to execute an innocent man named Rodney Reed. I am stopping everything in my life for these next 16 days to help save this man's life but I need your help. CLICK THE LINK IN MY BIO @ FreeRodneyReed.com, sign our petition, join our emergency team, and let's save this man's life. I've never been more sure that this nation was about to execute an innocent man than I am right now. We need you! Go to FreeRodneyReed.com now!

I knew the odds were stacked against Rodney and those of us fighting for him. And to be honest, I felt there was a chance that we might not make it. But I also needed to know that we had done everything we could to stop the execution.

Our goal was to get 100,000 people to sign the petition by the end of the first week. I built the petition with Jin Ding, an absolutely indispensable leader with the Action PAC, because we wanted full access to the email addresses and zip codes of every person who signed up. As a result, Jin was able to sync the signatures to a Google spreadsheet so we could track in real time how many were pouring in. Within twelve hours, more than 75,000 people had signed. We could barely believe it; I was practically jumping for joy.

We then signed into Mailchimp, our email service, so we could contact everyone with specific action steps for what to do next. Jin had also smartly synced the Google spreadsheet to Mailchimp. Had she not done so, we would soon learn that it would've been disastrous. According to Mailchimp, it was not 75,000 but 562,688 people who had signed our petition for Rodney. And it was growing by over 10,000 people every two or three minutes.

At first, Jin and I thought we had been hacked. We could not explain the gap. I thought somebody might've used bots to flood our petition with fake email addresses. But what we quickly learned was that the Google spreadsheet simply could not keep up with the overwhelming volume of people joining our cause, but Mailchimp was still capturing it.

We had done petitions for decades, but had never seen anything like this.

By this point, we knew my social media posts had gone

viral, but didn't know the petition itself had gone super-viral as well. Rihanna, who had become a key supporter of my work, not only signed the petition but shared it with her massive network. So did the rappers Meek Mill, Pusha T, Busta Rhymes, LL Cool J, and T.I.; the supermodel Gigi Hadid; Questlove from The Roots; and dozens of other prominent actors, actresses, musicians, and artists. We continued to track the petition in real time, and within forty-eight hours, we exceeded one million signatures. By then, almost every single prominent Democratic candidate for president either shared the petition or mentioned Rodney's case. In five days, our petition had 2,322,112 signatures. Although Dr. Phil did two full-length episodes on the case, his videos about it on YouTube had only a few thousand views apiece. But they were brilliant and included very compelling experts and witnesses speaking out on behalf of Rodney's innocence, so we downloaded the videos from YouTube, edited them to the Instagram format, and shared them across my social media accounts, where they quickly amassed several million views.

I am equal parts embarrassed and outraged over what I'm about to tell you, but Lee and I have learned that in addition to warm, humanizing photos and videos about the people we are advocating for, nothing is more important than having multiple white male validators speak out in support of Black victims of police brutality or mass incarceration. We've grown to think that it's one of the four or five most important factors in our ability to gain widespread public sympathy for a case. We saw it with Botham Jean, when the white male chairman of PricewaterhouseCoopers, Tim

Ryan, spoke out for Botham, reinforcing how beloved he was at the company. In fact, Botham was respected by white men at every stage of his academic, religious, and professional life, to the point that several of them were willing to come out and speak on his behalf. Those white male validators who vouched for Botham's character and humanity made him a near impossible target for the types of spin and propaganda that normally come out of local police departments after an officer kills someone. It's sad to say this, but those white validators made Botham, whose integrity was impeccable without them, palatable to the American mainstream in a way that we otherwise could not.

We saw the same thing in Texas when a white police officer named Roy Oliver shot and killed a brilliant, beautiful, unarmed, nonviolent, law-abiding fifteen-year-old Black boy named Jordan Edwards. Jordan was as close to perfect as any boy could be, but Lee and I had witnessed police and prosecutors smear boys just like him before. It was only when Jordan's white male football coaches and teachers and community leaders began speaking out about his impeccable character and integrity that we knew the wider public, especially there in Texas, would listen. And they did.

Dr. Phil McGraw, who lived and worked in Texas for decades, was the perfect white male validator for Rodney Reed. He flooded his episodes about Rodney with almost nothing but additional white male validators, ranging from attorneys, detectives, doctors, and more. It's a hard pill to swallow, but that testimony really mattered in those first few days of sharing Rodney's story.

In ten days, nearly three million people signed the petition, making it the single largest petition in the history of this country for a person on death row. We then pivoted to the next stage of our strategy: getting those energized people organized in strategic ways.

We set up five phone numbers for people to call, and designed it so that when they called in, the first voice they heard was mine, explaining step by step what we were about to do and whom they were going to speak to after we connected them. I impressed on them the importance of being passionate but polite and of keeping the mission for justice in the forefront during their calls. After my instructions, callers could press star on their phones, and we'd connect them to the first political office on the call. After that call was done, we'd transfer them to the next office, always giving a little pep talk and reminder of their mission between calls, until they made their way through the list.

So often people get scared at the idea of making phone calls to advocate for change, but liking social media posts or clicking angry-face emojis does nothing. It takes personal advocacy — strong, fierce, strategic advocacy — to change laws. We wanted to make it as easy as possible for people to overcome any nervous energy they had about calling to advocate for Rodney.

Behind the scenes, for the first time in my life, our staff consulted conservative Republican lobbyists and advisers for guidance on how we could best get conservatives on board. Because the truth was this: every key decision-maker in the process of stopping Rodney's execution was a Republican. On an average day, they would be my political adversaries, but now we needed them. Soon, several bipartisan groups of Republican and Democratic state legislators signed emergency public letters to Governor Abbott asking him to stop the execution. Conservative Republican senator Ted Cruz even wrote public statements advising that the execution be stopped. At a time when hyper-partisanship has caused some of the deepest divides in modern American history, people from all over the political spectrum were coming together to advocate for this execution to be stopped.

In the middle of all of this, our team joined the family of Rodney Reed for an emergency rally on the steps of the Texas Governor's Mansion in Austin. This time, and for the first time in my organizing life, I asked my wife and three youngest children to travel with me to the rally. Not only were they supportive of the work, they wanted to help however they could. It was a profound moment for me to have my babies see and hear me speak and understand more of what I do to advocate for people. For our safety, my wife and I try not to travel to high-risk public events together with our kids, but we felt this case warranted an exception, and so Rai and my three youngest flew down with me.

Rodney's family had held vigils and rallies for over twenty years, but attendance was normally twenty to thirty people at most—sometimes only two or three people would show up. This rally had close to a thousand people, not just from Texas but from all over the country, who drove or flew to Austin to support the cause.

As soon as we saw each other, Rodney's mother, Sandra, and I hugged and fought back tears. "I can't believe you are here," she said. "For years, it seemed like nobody even cared about us, or about Rodney, so to have you here with us just means so much to me." Soon afterward, Lee arrived from Houston, and she hugged us both like we were her sons. Over the next hour, out of the blue, she would grab our hands, squeeze them lovingly, and thank us more than we deserved.

Lee and I held a press conference with the family for the dozens of reporters who had shown up, and then we prepared to lead the rally. It was perfectly sunny and nearly eighty degrees that day—a far cry from the wintery cold in New York. A local pastor began the rally with a powerful prayer, and he then introduced Rodney's brother, Rodrick, who handed over the microphone to me. As I approached the podium, with Lee behind me, Rodrick on one side and Sandra on the other, I looked out at the beautiful crowd that had gathered for Rodney and had to hold in my feelings, thinking of all the families I had fought for over the years who never got this opportunity.

After I spoke, and quickly said goodbye to Lee and Rodney's family, we had to rush out to catch a flight for two more events that I was doing in California that evening. I wasn't ready for how emotional it made me when my kids EZ, Savannah, and Zayah told me how they intently listened and understood everything I had talked about—and how they had put their fists in the air and chanted "Free Rodney Reed" like everybody else.

Everywhere I traveled, people told me that they had signed the petition and were making calls to help stop Rodney's execution. I felt energy in the air, but I knew we had to keep pushing.

In total, our volunteers made hundreds of thousands of

phone calls to political offices. While the calls were coming in, our organizing team at the Action PAC helped petition signers start nearly two hundred vigils and rallies across the country. Our goal was for them to be held the Sunday before Rodney's scheduled execution, which had been set for Wednesday, November 20. Experts had advised us that they believed Governor Abbott was likely to wait until the very last day to make his decision.

On Friday, November 15, I put my phone on airplane mode during a doctor's appointment. When I left the office and switched my phone back on, I saw at least twenty texts messages:

Did you see the news?

Are you going to make an announcement?

Does that mean he'll get a new trial?

I had no idea what I had missed during the forty-five-minute appointment, but I knew it was damn important. As I read through all of the texts, I saw several updates from the team at the Innocence Project.

The deeply conservative Texas Board of Pardons and Paroles had unanimously voted to recommend that Governor Greg Abbott stop the execution in order to consider new evidence that could exonerate Rodney Reed.

My body filled with a lightness — this was the very organization we had made tens of thousands of calls to. I bet many of you reading this right now were among those callers. Every call, every email, every text, every signature on the petition mattered.

It was still up to the governor to accept or deny their recommendation, but this was, far and away, the best news we had ever received for Rodney. Surely, we thought, the governor would not ignore the unanimous recommendation of his own board. Immediately, I began letting my team know that we couldn't let up and that we would need to put as much pressure on the governor as we could. Then, less than an hour later, I got a call from Rodney's attorney, Bryce. Before the governor could even make his decision, the Texas Court of Criminal Appeals, another deeply conservative body, voted to intercede in the case to grant Rodney Reed an appeal. I was in such a state of shock, that I did not quite believe it. The legalese around the announcement was so dense that Bryce had to translate it for me over the phone.

"Shaun," he said, "they stopped the execution. There is no longer a date scheduled. We have been granted the opportunity to make an appeal."

As those words sunk in, the relief I felt coursing through my body was palpable. But I need to be clear: It was not joy. It was not celebratory. It was relief. All the tension I had stored up in my body those days, advocating for Rodney, and the years fighting for Eric, Michael, Tamir, Sandra, and too many others, began to loosen. It was a sliver of light, of hope, of the possibility of justice.

How much lower can a government go than executing someone who is not guilty of the crime they were convicted of? Studies estimate that anywhere from 2 percent to 10 percent of all convicted people are not guilty of the crimes they were sent to prison for. Maybe that doesn't sound like a lot to you, but when you think about the millions of people in prison in the United States, that means anywhere from 50,000 to 250,000 innocent people are in prison today. It takes my breath away. Any country that wrongly convicts that many people is in a dip. We might not have freed all of them, but we did just stop an execution. We were energized, organized, and approached the problem with a sophisticated plan that was mapped out with every key decision-maker and influencer we could think of. We worked that plan like a man's life depended on it, and together we were able to make change.

As I write this, Rodney Reed is alive. And I certainly hope and pray that he will still be alive when you are reading this. What I do know is that our efforts to save him are positive proof that it is absolutely possible to shift systems, to up-end the status quo. When you bring energized people, organized people, and a clear plan together, it gives you the very best chance to make change. And if you do all of those things and give it your best shot and you still fail, you will have the peace of mind of knowing that you did everything in your power to make a difference. If by chance Rodney doesn't make it, he will know, we will know, that we fought like hell to save his life.

For all of the setbacks and losses that I have experienced, that *we* have experienced, my hope remains. For most of the first three decades of my life, I had a youthful, foolish hope that the world was always positively marching forward, even if it hit some roadblocks along the way. But I have come to understand that's simply not how the world works. Time is full of peaks and valleys, highs and lows, progress and failure. But those highs and lows are made by us—which means we each have the ability to make an impact.

It's on us.

My final words to you are these: I believe in you. I truly do. I believe in your heart. I believe in your mind. I believe in your will. I believe in your determination. And I am counting on you to step up and serve.

I am asking you to act on your heart.

I am asking you now to live your life in such a way that your beliefs and your actions mirror each other so closely that we can't see where one begins and the other ends.

I am asking you to make the most serious commitment to systemic change that you've ever made in your life. And I am asking you to make it a lifelong commitment.

I am asking you to bring everybody you know and love with you.

Because this is it. This is our life. And together we can make change.

I'll see you on the journey.

# Acknowledgments

*A love letter to the friends and family who encouraged me, defended me, protected me, taught me, challenged me, and never bailed, no matter how hard it got.*

Writing, editing, and publishing a book is so much harder than the average reader ever understands. All they see is the finished product, but it took so many people to pull this off, and I am so amazingly grateful for each of them.

Rai, I have no idea who or what I'd be without you. I don't wanna know! We've been together since we were kids, and your steadfast love and support has everything to do with why I'm a leader today. I could write a whole book about our love. Maybe that's next?

Mom, you're the best mother a guy like me could ever have. I don't have a single memory from birth until now without you in my corner encouraging and supporting me every step of the way. I'm not sure I ever would've made it out of Versailles, Kentucky, without you in my ear, telling me that I was special.

My babies! I love you all so much. I know that no matter

what the world thinks or feels about me, you will always be there. Being your dad is such an honor. I hope the stories and lessons I shared here help make up for all the time this book took away from us.

Lee—my homie. It's on us. So glad to have a friend and brother to share this journey with. Until the wheels fall off, bro!

Lyssandra: This book would not exist without you micromanaging every single minute of my life. Thank you for making sure that I stayed on track until we got to the finish line.

Kate! Thank you for being the most understanding and thorough editor I could ever ask for. You've made this book so much better. Please send Liz, Fariza, Jenny, Katie, Christopher, Taryn, Michael, and the entire team my love.

Mel! Thank you for believing in me and convincing me that I deserved a first-class book deal—then making it happen!

Bernie! You are my hero. Having you write the foreword to this book was one of the single biggest honors of my life. Thank you for welcoming me into your family and network as we fight to make change together.

To all of my online friends on Instagram, Twitter, Facebook, and email: You've heard me say this so many times. I don't see you as numbers or clicks, but as real people, joining me in this work, determined to change the world. Thank you so much for your support every step of the way.

To all of the Real Justice staff, volunteers, and donors! Fighting alongside you to change our cruel and corrupt systems from the inside out has been an incredible honor.

Becky, thank you so much for thinking of me and inviting me to join you in this work.

To the staff and members of *The North Star*! Let's continue to use journalism to fight for freedom and dismantle systems of oppression. Thank you for enduring my time away every day as I wrote this book. You are the best!

To all of the Action PAC staff, volunteers, and donors! I am so proud of each of you and of what we've already been able to accomplish together to make the world a better place. You take my ideas and make them into action plans that make a real difference.

I have so many other people I'd like to thank. Please just know, if you've ever helped me along the way, I am grateful.

Lastly, I want to thank my dear brother, Jason. I had just started writing this book when cancer stole you from us. I love and miss you so very much. We all do. Nobody encouraged me more behind the scenes than you. You believed in all of my work and showed it with your actions.

# Index